FOUND MEALS

of the

LOST GENERATION

Found Meals

OF THE

Lost Generation

RECIPES AND ANECDOTES

FROM 1920S PARIS

*

Suzanne Rodriguez-Hunter

Faber and Faber

BOSTON • LONDON

First paperback edition published in 1997.
Copyright © 1994 by Suzanne Rodriguez-Hunter

Library of Congress Cataloging-in-Publication Data

Rodriguez-Hunter, Suzanne.
    Found meals of the lost generation : recipes and anecdotes from 1920s Paris / Suzanne Rodriguez-Hunter.
        p.   cm.
    Includes bibliographical references.
    ISBN 0-571-19925-9
    1. Dinners and dining—France—Paris. 2. Cookery. 3. Authors—Homes and haunts—France—Paris. 5. Paris (France)—Social life and customs—20th century. 6. Americans—France—Paris—History—20th century. I. Title.
TX737.R63   1994
641.5944—dc20   ·94-19214
                                                            CIP

Jacket illustration and design by Jane Mjølsness
Printed in the United States of America

This book is for my parents. In your heart of hearts I know you both preferred my first Life Plan—becoming a lawyer—but you've nonetheless always been incredibly supportive of my writing. Thanks for that.

Dinners, soirées, poets, erratic millionaires, transla-
tions, lobsters, absinthe, music, promenades, oysters,
sherry, aspirin, pictures, Sapphic heiresses, editors,
books, sailors. And how!

—Hart Crane, in a 1929 postcard from Paris

There are many ways of eating, for some eating is living, for some eating is dying, for some thinking about
ways of eating gives to them the feeling that they have
it in them to be alive and to be going on living....

—Gertrude Stein

If you are lucky enough to have lived in Paris as a
young man, then wherever you go for the rest of your
life, it stays with you, for Paris is a moveable feast.

—Ernest Hemingway

CONTENTS

INTRODUCTION

*F*ound *Meals of the Lost Generation*—a book about the 1920s American expatriate scene in Paris—is social history with recipes, a kind of edible time machine. Each chapter devotes itself to a major literary or artistic figure of the day and finishes with a contemporary quotation describing an actual meal in which he or she took part. Twenties-style recipes, also included, allow you to fix the very same meal. With a bit of imagination, you'll soon be sharing steak-frites with Hemingway on the Ile St. Louis, attending formal tea in the living room of Gertrude Stein, sitting over cold supper with Sylvia Beach and James Joyce, eating lobster backstage at the Follies with Josephine Baker, or sipping champagne with Isadora Duncan.

The idea for this book was born during a year I spent living in Paris. Like many others with a literary bent and a passion for the expats, I often toured the Montparnasse hot spots of yesteryear. I dallied on the sidewalk before the ancient building where Ernest and Hadley Hemingway first lived in 1921, that place above the *bal musette*; peered over the fence at 20, rue Jacob, trying to catch a glimpse of

Natalie Barney's Temple à l'Amitié; sat for hours sipping un café at the Select, a favorite late-night haunt of Bob McAlmon and Kay Boyle; stood outside 27, rue de Fleurus, imagining Gertrude Stein's studio hung floor to ceiling with the most explosive art of the century.

This was all great fun, but something was missing: I was on the outside looking in. Much as I'd like to, I'd never be able to travel back in time for a wild night on the town with, say, Man Ray and Kiki. I resigned myself to this fact until one day I stumbled onto a way I could participate here and now with there and then.

One of the places I discovered through my trusty walking-tour guidebook was Au Pont Marie, a restaurant close to my home on the Ile St. Louis. In the twenties, when it was Au Rendezvous-des-Mariniers, it was owned by the charming Mme. Le Comte. The Rendezvous had an outstanding reputation among Americans for good food and modest prices (frequent diners were John Dos Passos, Robert McAlmon, Sherwood Anderson, Harry Crosby and Virgil Thomson).

Hemingway liked the restaurant and its owner so much that he put them both in *The Sun Also Rises*. Reading on the quai one lazy afternoon almost seventy years after *Sun*'s publication, I came across that passage, the one in which Jake Barnes and his friend Bill eat roast chicken and joke with Mme. Le Comte.

I grabbed a friend, and soon we were sitting in the former Rendezvous munching on roast chicken and talking about our favorite Hemingway characters. Afterward we walked around the island, following the identical path taken by Jake and Bill.

That experience was the genesis of *Found Meals*. I knew there had to be other expatriate meals detailed by participants in memoirs or fictionalized accounts, and so I started searching. Many of the books weren't easily available, and many had been long out of print, but they were there. I just had to find them—find the meals of the lost generation. When I did I recreated them in my kitchen, re-populating them with my friends.

My intent in writing *Found Meals* has been this: to share my love of a particular era with others; to make that era come alive by introducing the people who lived it; to provide a means of symbolically re-living the time; and to have fun in the process. I think I've succeeded with the first three goals, and I know damn well I have with the fourth.

Ernest Hemingway was right: Paris *is* a moveable feast. Have fun and *bon appétit!*

A NOTE ABOUT THE RECIPES

Recipes are as faithful as possible to the 1920s. There are thus no references to food processors, blenders, etc. As in the twenties, ingredients are not listed separately.

Whenever possible, I've used a recipe derived from an identifiable 1920s source (give or take a decade). That information will always be contained with the recipe.

All recipes serve four unless otherwise indicated.

THE LOST GENERATION

They rebelled against their parents, danced to loud and shocking music, were disillusioned by war, flirted with cocaine, pushed the boundaries of sexual freedom, cut their hair geometrically and colored it with henna, loved abstract art, joined cults, flew in airplanes in a world grown small, drove fast cars, pondered their subconscious motivations, rejected conformism, and a lot of them drank or drugged too much.

If you didn't know better you'd think they were baby boomers, especially the ones who came of age in the sixties, but you'd be wrong. They were the Moderns—the first modern generation. Born around the turn of this century, they are known to us now as the Lost Generation.*

Their elders came from a far different and much slower world. At the century's start almost everyone journied by

---

*It was actually Gertrude Stein who gave the younger generation this name. Vexed by an action of Hemingway's, she told him: "That's what you all are ... all of you young people who served in the war. You are a lost generation." The remark itself might have been lost if Hemingway hadn't used it on the title page of *The Sun Also Rises*. As the book's popularity grew, the term "Lost Generation" passed into legend.

horse or train. The automobile had arrived, but it was unreliable, expensive, and difficult to use: there were few paved roads outside the cities, and certainly no gas stations. Radio hadn't yet been invented. Phones existed but were scarce, used mostly in business. Fashion for women dictated floor-dusting skirts, corsets, and high-collared shirtwaists; even casually dressed men wore starched collars, stiff shirts, three-piece suits, and hats. The tallest building in the country, the Ivins Syndicate in New York City, was twenty-nine stories high. As there was little electricity, most people read by gas lamp. Refrigerated railway cars existed but were ineffective; fresh fruits and vegetables were thus scarce or unavailable in much of the country from autumn to spring. Most people lived in homes with outdoor toilets. A fifth of all children under fifteen worked ten-hour days.

Born with the new century, the Lost Generation experienced great changes: the rise of a huge middle class, reform movements, womens' demand for and eventual winning of the vote, Freud's theories of the subconscious, Margaret Sanger's birth control clinics, the invention of the airplane, the popularization of moving pictures and movie stars, the rise of sports heroes, and the introduction of income tax.

And, of course, the automobile. With the introduction of the Model T in 1908, the automobile—now affordable by most—began its swift reshaping of American geography. Suddenly gas stations were everywhere and paved roads connected towns and villages. Interstate highways abounded, overcrowded parking lots dotted cities, automobile fatalities rose, and suburbs sprang up like mushrooms in a spring rain. More insidious were the social changes provoked by the auto, especially for young people. Introduced to speed and mobility, they could escape from prying parental eyes. No longer forced to court on the front porch, their sexual values changed: young women from San Jose to Greenwich Village sought sexual freedom, and young men were happy to oblige.

By the closing of the century's second decade, youthful rebellion had been intensified by other factors, particularly a meanly fought war that killed nearly ten million. Those who survived World War I had endured poison gas, putrefying corpses, mass destruction, filth, and starvation. America—with its Puritan values and Rotary Clubs— seemed unreal from the battlefield. "At present America is to me utter anathema," John Dos Passos confided to his diary from the trenches in 1917. "I can't think of it without belching disgust at the noisiness of it, the meaningless chatter of its lying tongues."

Many returning soldiers found American life empty of meaning and looked back at Europe with longing. Harry Crosby, who had served as an ambulance driver in the thick of battle, found postwar America bleak and depressing:

> Red drug-stores, filling stations, comfort stations, go-to-the-right signs, lurid billboards and automobiles swarming everywhere like vermin over a charogne. A clean emptiness, an atmosphere of frus-

tration, disillusion and a great many unimportant things and unimportant people. How I hate this community spirit with its civic federations and its boyscout clubs and its educational toys and its Y.M.C.A. and its congregational baptist churches and all this smug self-satisfaction.

"The only thing left in which we could believe was art," wrote the poet Bryher years later. "If it were to fill the hollow left by chaos, [it] must be revolutionary and new. It must find words that were not tainted by nineteenth-century associations, rhythms that fitted the purr of machines rather than the thudding of hooves, different colors and, above all, a sternly truthful approach."

Where else to find the new but in Paris, the capital of Modernism? From there had already come the cubism of Picasso and Braque, the ballets of Diaghilev, the liberating movement of Isadora Duncan, the streamlined sculpture of Brancusi, the atonal music of Erik Satie, the discordant sounds of Stravinsky, and the radical writing of Stein and Joyce.

And so the Lost Generation came to Paris to participate in the most vibrant artistic explosion of the twentieth century.

Some came to create music, and we now have Gershwin's *An American in Paris*, Antheil's *Ballet Mécanique*, Thomson's *Four Saints in Three Acts*, and Porter's "Paree, What Did You Do to Me?"

Some came to be poets, giving us the earliest works of e. e. cummings, Archibald MacLeish, Langston Hughes, and Virgil Geddes, as well as the last works of Hart Crane and Harry Crosby.

Two—Isadora Duncan and Josephine Baker—came to dance; though their styles were polar extremes, the legends they left are alike in mythical proportion.

Some, like William Shirer, Janet Flanner, A. J. Liebling, and Waverley Root, came to be journalists; each would reach the pinnacle of that profession.

Some came to work in the visual arts, and so we have the photographs and films of Man Ray; the paintings of Gerald Murphy; and the early works of Stuart Davis, Jo Davidson, and Alexander Calder.

But above all, some came to write fiction, and they wrote on a grand scale: from their time in Paris has come much of the great American literature of this century— Hemingway's *The Sun Also Rises* and *A Farewell to Arms*, Fitzgerald's *Tender Is the Night*, Dos Passos's *The U.S.A. Trilogy*, Barnes's *Nightwood*, Pound's *Cantos*, and Stein's *The Making of Americans*.

In the following pages you'll meet many of the people who lived in Paris during this rollicking, exhilarating decade of creativity. You'll find them a disparate group: small-town and big-city, rich and poor, straight and gay. Many went to Harvard or Princeton; others barely made it through high school. Few were sober. One, Natalie Barney, lived to be a joyous ninety-six; another, Harry Crosby, committed suicide at thirty-one.

They were young, and they were trying to find themselves. They were, after all, the Lost Generation.

1900–1909

1900 Publication of Natalie Barney's first book, *Quelques Portraits et Sonnets de Femmes*... *1903* Gertrude Stein takes up residence at 27, rue de Fleurus; she is twenty-nine ... Constantin Brancusi arrives in Paris; he is twenty-seven... *1905* The Steins buy their first Matisse, *Femme au Chapeau*, and first Picasso, *Jeune Fille aux Fleurs*... Alfred Stieglitz founds Photo-Secession Gallery at 291 Fifth Avenue in New York; over next few years the gallery introduces America to the world's most progressive painting and sculpture, including works by Cézanne, Matisse, Brancusi, Picasso, Braque, and Rodin... *1908* Picasso's banquet for Henri Rousseau... *1909* First year of Natalie Barney's literary salon at 20, rue Jacob; she is thirty-three ... First Paris performance of Diaghilev's Russian Ballet...

PICASSO, GERTRUDE STEIN, AND HENRI ROUSSEAU:
The Feast Begins

S hortly after the turn of the century, in a seedy part
of Montmartre, a group of young, impoverished
writers and painters inhabited a ramshackle collection of buildings known as the Bateau Lavoir. They were a
tight and tiny avant garde, downing their daily apéritifs at
the nearby Lapin Agile, dancing alongside gangsters at the
infamous *bals musettes*, sometimes combining resources
to throw a party.

Only once, however—on a fall night in 1908—did they
hold a banquet. By 1920 this event had taken on mytho-
logical proportions for a younger generation of writers
and artists, because many of that banquet's guests had
grown famous, vital to twenties Paris and integral to the
experience of the Lost Generation. This banquet, given by
Picasso for the painter Henri Rousseau, was the precursor
to all the meals that follow in this book.

Rousseau, who was sixty-four in 1908, had exhibited
without success for much of his life. A contemporary of
the Impressionists, his style—naïve, primitive, evoking a
strange and original world—was often derided by the

public, critics, and even other artists. But with the new century came a younger generation of painters rebelling against the Impressionists, whose work they considered decorative and passé, illustrative of a dead century.

Although these young artists considered Rousseau an amateur (he'd never taken an art lesson), they nonetheless applauded his audacious imagination and bizarre vision. So it was that the old man was befriended by young lions such as Picasso, Fernand Léger, Guillaume Apollinaire, and Robert Delaunay. Rousseau, whose belief in his art had never wavered, took the attention in stride. He once told Picasso, his junior by more than forty years, "We are the greatest artists, you in the Egyptian style, I in the modern."

Picasso purchased his first Rousseau in the fall of 1908. Browsing one day in a junk shop, he came across a large painting of a woman standing beside a window. The dealer didn't think much of *Portrait of a Woman*, and sold it to the young Spaniard for five francs (about one dollar), adding that the canvas could be painted over and re-used. But Picasso knew he'd found a bargain and decided to celebrate his purchase by honoring its creator.*

He asked thirty friends to a banquet, among them the painters George Braque and Marie Laurencin; the writers André Salmon and Guillaume Apollinaire; and the Ameri-

---

Portrait of a Woman, worth millions today, can be seen at the Musée Picasso, Paris. Works by Rousseau are in the collections of most major modern art museums, including New York's Museum of Modern Art and the Musée d'Orsay in Paris.

cans Gertrude Stein, her brother Leo, and her new friend Alice B. Toklas. The guests were to gather in Montmartre for an apéritif at the Bar Fauvet with its new coin-operated electric organ. At eight o'clock they would march up-hill to Picasso's big barn of a studio, settle down, and prepare to greet Rousseau when he arrived a short while later.

Then would come the feast, a riz à la Valenciennes prepared by Picasso's girlfriend, Fernande Olivier, with accompanying dishes provided by Félix Potin, a grocer specializing in prepared food. Later would be toasts to Rousseau, followed by songs and poetry. All in all, a dignified tribute.

But the evening didn't turn out as intended. Accounts vary wildly (it was a very drunken evening), and so the following composite contains events that may or may not have occurred, depending on whose story you believe:*

At the Bar Fauvet, the normally discreet Marie Laurencin consumed way too many apéritifs. She grew noisy and giddy, jumping onto chairs and singing loudly. Attention was diverted from her momentarily when Fernande burst in, angry and upset because the prepared dishes from Potin hadn't arrived and the store was now closed. Alice Toklas offered to help Fernande find a grocer, and

---

*Eyewitness accounts have been written by Fernande Olivier, André Salmon, Gertrude Stein, Leo Stein, Maurice Raynal, Alice Toklas, and André Warnod.

The Feast Begins

the two women left hurriedly. But, as the local grocers had rolled up their shutters for the night, Fernande was reluctantly forced to make do with the riz à la Valenciennes and a few desserts. She returned to her preparations at Picasso's studio, and Alice rejoined Gertrude in the bar.

Soon the group left Fauvet's and set out for the Bateau Lavoir. By now Laurencin was so drunk she could barely walk. Gertrude and Leo supported her with their comfortable bulk and pushed her, bouncing back and forth between them, all the way up the hill. At the studio Fernande took one look at Laurencin and dramatically barred the door. Gertrude announced that she'd "be hanged if after the struggle of getting Marie Laurencin up that terrific hill it was going to be for nothing." Picasso agreed, overruling Fernande. Laurencin entered the room and promptly fell into a tray of jam tarts.

The studio was outfitted with carpenter's trestles and boards for tables, and long wooden benches for seats. The place of honor was a rickety wooden chair set atop a crate. Behind the head table was Picasso's new acquisition, *Portrait of a Woman,* framed by flags and wreaths. African masks decorated the walls (Picasso had recently embarked on Cubism, which was greatly influenced by primitive art), and the beams were strung with garlands and Chinese lanterns. Stacked in corners were dozens of Picasso's paintings. Everyone took a seat and awaited Rousseau's arrival.

Finally came a tentative knock on the door. Rousseau

entered slowly, carrying his ubiquitous cane in one hand and his violin in the other. Old enough to be grandfather to the others, the kind, frail old man stood awkwardly, glancing hesitantly about. He took it all in: the formal seating, his painting on the wall, the place of honor. He had struggled most of his life for recognition and acceptance by other artists, and at that moment, two years before his death, had finally found it. There was a long, emotional silence as he stood in the doorway with tears in his eyes. Finally he moved to the place of honor and conversation resumed.

The feast commenced. Picasso had contributed fifty bottles of wine to the evening and everyone else brought additions, so the meal, though scant, was well oiled. Marie Laurencin continued drinking and acting the fool until her lover Apollinaire hauled her downstairs; when they returned she was, according to Gertrude Stein, "a little bruised but sober." Hungry neighbors dropped by and swiped the petits fours. A character from the nearby tavern, Lapin Agile, wandered in with his donkey, Lolo. Both were given a drink and left, but not before Lolo ate Alice Toklas's flowered hat. A group of Italian street singers joined in the fun but were escorted out by Fernande, who was trying in vain to keep the banquet "respectable." There were toasts, and then Apollinaire read a poem he'd written to Rousseau, which ended with a rousing refrain:

Nous sommes réunis pour célébrer ta gloire
Ces vins qu'en ton honneur nous verse Picasso

Buvons-les donc, puisque c'est l'heure de les boire
*En criant tous en choeur: "Vive! Vive Rousseau!"**

And then, according to Gertrude Stein (who some-times wrote about herself in the third person):

all of a sudden André Salmon who was sitting next to my friend and solemnly discoursing of literature and travels, leaped upon the by no means solid table and poured out an extemporaneous eulogy and poem. At the end he seized a big glass and drank what was in it, then promptly went off his head, being completely drunk, and began to fight. The men all got hold of him, the statues tottered, Braque, a great big chap, got hold of a statue in either arm and stood there holding them while Gertrude Stein's brother another big chap, protected little Rousseau and his violin from harm. The others with Picasso leading because Picasso though small is very strong, dragged Salmon into the front atelier and locked him in.

When everything calmed down, Rousseau played on the violin a waltz he'd written, "Clémence," named for his first wife. Laurencin, sober now, sang old Norman songs, and the painter Pichot performed a religious Spanish

---

*We are gathered to celebrate your glory/Picasso is pouring us wine in your honor/Therefore let us drink, for it's time to drink/Crying all together, "Hurrah! Hurrah for Rousseau!"

dance in which he thrashed about and ended up stretched on the floor like a crucified Christ. Braque played the accordian with inebriated gusto. Apollonaire asked Gertrude and Alice to sing American Indian songs but they didn't know any. The corner barman came by to say that one of the lady guests had rolled down the hill into a gutter and he couldn't get her up. Rousseau fell asleep under a lantern that dripped hot wax on his head, forming into a small cone, but after a while he woke up and began his entire repertoire of songs all over again.

Gertrude and Alice took Rousseau home in a horse-drawn carriage sometime around three in the morning. According to Alice's own account, as the carriage drew away Salmon came running down the hill screaming and then raced past them until he disappeared into the darkness.

The rest of the guests stayed until dawn, although no one seems to remember much about the last few hours. "It was impossible for anyone who remained to say exactly how the party ended," wrote André Warnod, "for we had been very thirsty and the eau-de-vie was plentiful."

*

The Feast Begins

The Found Meal for The Modernists

Riz à la Valenciennes

This dish is based on a recipe of the painter Henri de Toulouse-Lautrec contained in his cookbook, *The Art of Cuisine.*

Cut a generous handful of string beans into 3-inch pieces and simmer in water until crisp; you should have about 1 cup. Drain and plunge string beans into cold water; retain cooking water. Strip tough outside leaves from 3 artichokes; simmer in water until barely done; cut each into 4 pieces and remove chokes. Peel 2 large tomatoes and squeeze to remove seeds. Steam 2 dozen clams and mussels just until open; remove meat, discarding shells but retaining shellfish liquid.

Brown 4 large or 8 small pieces of chicken in olive oil in a round paella pan. Remove chicken when well browned. Sauté large onion and 2 chopped cloves of garlic in same pan, gathering up brown bits. Add 2 cups rice and 4 cups liquid made from string bean cooking water and shellfish liquid (add extra water if necessary). Salt and pepper to taste. Add chicken, tomatoes, and artichokes, stirring to mix all ingredients.

Let cook over low flame; don't cover or stir contents.

When liquid has almost disappeared, gently add shelled mussels, clams, and string beans. When liquid has evaporated, rice will be done. Sprinkle strips of green and red peppers, lightly sautéed in olive oil, on top. Serve directly from pan.

Tartes de Confiture à la Marie Laurencin

Make a pâté brisée by cutting with a fork 12 ounces chilled unsalted butter into 3 cups unsifted flour mixed with 2 teaspoons salt and ¼ teaspoon sugar. When mixture has oatmeal texture, add ¾ to 1 cup ice water, forming a dough. Roll dough into a ball, cover with waxed paper, and allow to rest in refrigerator for at least 30 minutes. Keeping the dough cold and working quickly, roll out to ⅛-inch thickness and line individual tartlet pans. Prick all over with a fork and fill tartlets with dried beans to keep the dough in place during baking. Bake in a preheated 425° oven for 10 to 15 minutes. Remove from oven, unmold, and cool on rack.

For each tartlet choose 1 or more pieces of drained fruit compote (cherries, apricots, peaches or pineapple) or fresh berries (strawberries or rasberries) and arrange nicely in tartlet shell. Heat red currants or sieved apricot jam and glaze the fruits with a thin coating of jam.

Suggested Wine

Red Spanish wine such as a Riojas, or a hearty French burgundy.

1910–1919

1911 Publication of Djuna Barnes's *Book of Repulsive Women*... *1913* New York Armory Show introduces modern art to American public; showstopper is Duchamp's *Nude Descending a Staircase*... In Paris, Stravinsky's *Le Sacre du Printemps* premieres with Diaghilev's Russian Ballet; audience riots... Brassière invented by Caresse Crosby, née Mary Jacobs... First issue of Margaret Anderson's *Little Review*... James Joyce begins writing *Ulysses*... *1916* Sylvia Beach arrives in Paris; she is twenty-eight... *1917* The United States enters European War in April... *1919* Shakespeare and Company opens in Paris... First meeting of poets H.D. and Bryher... Dada at its height of popularity... John Dos Passos arrives in Paris, writes *Three Soldiers*...

GERTRUDE STEIN AND ALICE B. TOKLAS:
The Road Kill

I n the Beginning there was Gertrude Stein. She had always been there, squatting heavy and Buddha-like in her studio at 27, rue de Fleurus, back-dropped by the century's most progressive art, surrounded by the famous and infamous, guarded jealously by Alice B. Toklas. There had never been a Paris without Stein, or a Stein without Paris—or so all this seemed to a younger generation arriving after the war.

But Stein's path to the Queenship of Modernism was a circuitous one, and unplanned. Born in 1874 in Pennsylvania, she grew up in Oakland, California. Later, while attending Radcliffe, she became friendly with the psychologist William James, who encouraged her to attend medical school. She did, enrolling in Johns Hopkins. She did well at first but in 1902, having grown bored—and having flunked many of her classes—she left.

Unsure what to do with her life, the next year she joined her elder brother Leo in Paris where he had settled in a two-story apartment with detached studio on rue de Fleurus. Life was pleasant and the dollar went far, so Stein stayed on. Thus began the second part of her life, "not the half that made me but the half in which I made what I made."

By the time Gertrude joined him, Leo had amassed a modest art collection consisting mainly of Japanese landscape prints. For some time, however, he had nurtured a growing interest in an entirely new form of art. Vaguely labeled Modernism, it was considered by most of his contemporaries to be shocking, vulgar, and very ugly. Shortly before Gertrude's arrival Leo made his first purchase of such a work, an early Cézanne landscape.

Leo's modernist fervor rubbed off on Gertrude, and soon the pair were frequently visiting the art dealer Ambroise Vollard, who had dozens of Cézannes in his back room. The Steins weren't rich; their monthly income of $150 each from a family trust was merely enough to let them live comfortably, and in order to buy paintings they economized where they could. Their chief saving was in clothing. They dressed simply, in plain brown corduroy and sandals, and counseled other impecunious art collectors to do the same.* Vollard once said that the Steins were the only clients he'd had who bought paintings "not because they were rich, but despite the fact that they weren't."

Soon the Steins amassed a collection of works by

---

*Stein once advised Ernest Hemingway's first wife, the pretty and stylish Hadley, to buy clothes for durability and comfort rather than style, using the money saved to buy pictures. Hemingway later recalled Hadley struggling, throughout this conversation, to avoid looking askance at Gertrude's strange clothing.

Renoir, Cézanne, and Gaugin. The latter two had few admirers and were largely unknown; the Steins' purchase of their work shows remarkable foresight. Not as much, however, as with their next two discoveries: Henri Matisse and Pablo Picasso.

The Steins' first Matisse was the revolutionary *Femme au Chapeau*, a work that, with its scorching brushwork and wild colors, created angry riots at the 1905 Autumn Salon. Gertrude and Alice befriended the dignified and scholarly Matisse, then barely eking out an existence, and continued buying his work; they were thus the great painter's first patrons. For a time they were frequent dinner companions of Matisse and his wife. "Gertrude Stein and her brother were often at the Matisses," Stein wrote, "and the Matisses were constantly with them."

One day, browsing in a shop, Leo came across an unusual painting of a young girl by an unknown Spaniard. He brought Gertrude to see it, and she hated it on sight. Leo bought it anyway, forcing Gertrude to live with Picasso's *Jeune Fille aux Fleurs*.

The painting grew on her, though, and when she and Picasso met soon thereafter they took to each other immediately. Gertrude thought him handsome and "thin dark, alive with big pools of eyes and a violent but not rough way." Soon Picasso was dining regularly at rue de Fleurus, and before long Gertrude was posing for his now-famous *Portrait of Gertrude Stein*.

By 1906 the Steins' small studio was hung—row upon

row, eye-level to ceiling—with works by Matisse, Picasso, Renoir, Cézanne, Delacroix, Maurice Denis, Henri Manguin, Felix Vallotton, Pierre Bonnard, and Henri Toulouse-Lautrec. Word of the collection got around, and people began coming by to take a look at what was perhaps the world's first museum of modern art. Eventually, besieged day and night by callers, the Steins reserved Saturday evenings for visitors to their collection.

And visit they did, by the hundreds: young painters and writers, collectors, journalists, friends, dealers, and the simply curious. Matisse and Picasso were usually there—they met for the first time at rue de Fleurus, in fact—and brought friends of their own. In this way the French avant-garde, including Apollinaire, Max Jacob, and Marie Laurencin, came into Gertrude's life.

At first Leo held center stage. He loved to pontificate, and the writer Mabel Dodge remembered him "always standing up before the canvases . . . with a fire no one would have suspected . . . expounding, teaching, interpreting."

While Leo presided over the hectic, noisy gatherings, Gertrude sat serenely and often silently, with monumental weight and dignity, like a rock-solid barn in the midst of a storm. When she spoke in her deep, slow voice, her words seemed heavy with significance: increasingly, people paused to listen. The fact that she often talked in riddles, loved spiteful gossip, and frequently praised her own genius, mattered little. Gertrude's physical solidity, bohemian eccentricities, and sensational collection of art and artists combined to give her a powerful, charismatic presence.

Before too long the inevitable happened: Gertrude eclipsed Leo, emerging as the star of the Saturday evenings. People now came not only to pay homage to the Stein art collection, but to Gertrude Stein herself.

There was more to Gertrude's life than running a salon, of course: she wrote. Though she hadn't yet achieved much success, it wasn't for lack of trying. She wrote prolifically each night, usually until dawn. Her first novel, *Q.E.D.*, drew on her experience in a lesbian relationship in Baltimore; when she finished it, she tucked it into a drawer where it remained until unearthed sometime in 1930 (it was finally published posthumously). *Three Lives*, self-published in 1909, sold only seventy-three copies in a year and a half, but drew good reviews.

It was when she began writing "word portraits" of her friends—trying, by use of repetition and lack of punctuation, to emulate cubism—that her work was widely noticed, though not always favorably. In 1909 Alfred Stieglitz published her word portrait of Matisse in *Camera Work*, where passages such as the following attracted controversy and derision:

He certainly very clearly expressed something. Some said that he did not clearly express anything. Some were certain that he expressed something very clearly and some of such of them said that he would have been a greater one if he had not been one so clearly expressing what he was expressing. Some said he was not clearly expressing what he was expressing and some of such of them said that the greatness of struggling which was not clear expression made of him one being a completely great one.

Margaret Anderson, editor of the *Little Review*, a literary magazine that showcased writers such as James Joyce, said of Stein's writing: "I for one still have difficulty, a difficulty that is often unrewarded by understanding. And my understanding is often unrewarded by interest." On the other hand, there were those—most notably the critics Carl Van Vechten and Henry McBride—who considered her a ground-breaker, a bold experimentalist bringing English literature into the modern world.

Upon such controversies are reputations made; Stein's was either quite good or very bad, depending on which critic you read, but it was *never* indifferent. Her portraits and poetry slowly found publication in the little magazines of the time. In 1912, *Tender Buttons*, a book of sketches said by Gertrude to reveal "the history of anything," was published in the United States. The book's cryptic sentences and eccentric syntax solidified her reputation as a literary innovator among some—and a hoax among others.* No matter the judgment, though, every-

---

*A *New York Post* reviewer wondered whether Gertrude had eaten hashish while writing *Tender Buttons*.

one agreed that Stein espoused the modern; her writing, together with her collection of paintings, proved that.

And more people than ever wanted to see those paintings. Visiting American artists—Marsden Hartley, Joseph Stella, Charles Demuth—brought back favorable word of the Stein collection, which in turn brought increasingly larger groups of curious visitors to rue de Fleurus. Van Vechten and McBride kept her name constantly before the public, giving her the nickname "the cubist of letters." Gertrude's name was often mentioned in newspaper and magazine coverage of the 1913 Armory Show, which introduced modern art to a largely uncomprehending American public. Just as most Americans did not understand cubism or *Nude Descending a Staircase* or Brancusi's straight lines, so were they at a loss when confronted with Gertrude's writing. A popular ditty at the time of the show summed it up:

> I called the canvas *Cow with cud*
> And hung it on the line,
> Altho' to me 'twas vague as mud,
> 'Twas clear to Gertrude Stein.

Gertrude Stein's name was now forever intertwined with Modernism. Though few had read her, everybody knew her name. Stein became one of the world's first media stars, famous for being famous.

In 1913 Leo left rue de Fleurus, taking most of the Matisses and Cézannes, and leaving all of the Picassos. His reasons for departing were many, but foremost among them was his jealousy of Alice Babette Toklas.

Alice, originally from San Francisco, came to live with Gertrude in 1910. The two had met a few years before that, and in short order the dark and exotic Toklas made herself indispensable. Each morning she typed up Stein's writing from the night before; she ran Gertrude's errands; she took over the household—hiring and firing servants, shopping, supervising the preparation of meals; and in general acted as Gertrude's factotum and secretary. Though self-effacing in public, she exerted her strong will on Gertrude in private. Theirs was a romance that would last a lifetime, ending only with Gertrude's death in 1946.

By World War I, Gertrude's Saturday nights had become a major draw for visiting Americans (one observer called Stein "an attraction like the bearded lady in the circus"). The war put a stop to all that. Gertrude bought a Ford truck, christened it *Auntie*, and took off with Alice to spend the war years delivering hospital supplies in southwest France. Food was scarce, sometimes nonexistent. Gertrude later recalled in *Paris France*, a short book extolling her love of that city, the lengths to which they sometimes resorted for a meal:

The Doctor Chaboux managed well he did not try but he did kill a hare with his automobile on the road and we were invited to eat it, with jugged hare you always have to eat boiled potatoes and really boiled potatoes and hare were very good. They say in the country here that potatoes are the healthiest of all foods, to be sure they do eat a great deal of bread as well as wine but after all, they say, you do give potatoes to sick people you do not give them bread, bread is for the strong, potatoes are for the healthy and the ill, but what really is important is that in this very country where the twentieth century was to be found and celebrated in the arts they still call them Mère Mollard, or the Père Mollard or the Fils Mollard and they call a painter who is old chèr maitre. They will do that. I cannot write too much upon how necessary it is to be completely conservative that is particularly traditional in order to be free. And so France is and was.

For their efforts during the war Gertrude and Alice each received the Médaille de la Reconnaissance Française. Pleased with the small part they'd played in the war to end all wars, they returned to 27, rue de Fleurus and prepared to greet the 1920s.

*

The Found Meal for Gertrude Stein and Alice B. Toklas

JUGGED HARE WITH RED CURRANT
JELLY-WINE SAUCE
BOILED POTATOES
WINE

Jugged hare was very popular in 1920s Europe. In *A Moveable Feast* Ernest Hemingway recalls eating it with his first wife, Hadley, on an Austrian skiing trip. In *The Autobiography of Alice B. Toklas*,* Stein mentions being served the dish quite often by Madame Matisse.

Jugged Hare

A recipe from *The Alice B. Toklas Cook Book* formed the basis of this recipe.

Cut a 5-pound rabbit or hare into pieces and place in deep bowl. In a separate bowl combine 1 cup red wine such as burgundy, ¼ cup red wine vinegar, 1 large onion cut into quarters, 2 sliced carrots, 1 bay leaf, 12 whole peppercorns, 4 sprigs parsley, 1½ teaspoons salt, and ½ teaspoon fresh ground pepper; stir ingredients well and pour over rabbit. If rabbit is not covered by mixture, add more wine. Cover and let marinate in refrigerator overnight.

Two hours before serving, drain rabbit mixture

---

*Despite the title, *Alice* was written by Stein.

through a colander, reserving marinade. Heat a small amount of olive oil in a large frying pan; sauté rabbit until browned on all sides. Remove to covered casserole. Sauté onions and carrots until soft in the same pan, adding a little olive oil if necessary; add vegetables to casserole. Deglaze the pan with 1 cup water and add reserved marinade to casserole. Place casserole, covered, in preheated 300° oven. Prepare a beurre manié by blending with a fork ¼ cup flour and 2 tablespoons softened butter; stir into the casserole after one hour. Return casserole to oven for another 30 to 45 minutes. Arrange rabbit on a serving platter, strain sauce over meat, and surround with boiled potatoes. Serve with red currant jelly-wine sauce.

Red Currant Jelly-Wine Sauce

Slowly heat 1 cup red currant jelly over medium fire; when runny, add 1 cup good red wine and 1 tablespoon lemon juice; mix well and simmer gently, uncovered, 5 minutes. Thicken to taste with sauce from the rabbit casserole. Just before serving, blend in 1 tablespoon brandy.

Boiled Potatoes

Wash thoroughly and peel 8 medium-sized potatoes (2 per person). Drop into large pot of boiling salted water; let cook until tender when pierced with a knife (approximately 30 minutes). Drain well. Return to pot, add 3 tablespoons melted butter and 4 tablespoons finely chopped parsley, and toss gently over a low flame until butter is melted and potatoes are coated. Remove to serving platter.

Suggested Wine

A Beaujolais or Côte de Rhone would go nicely with this dish.

JOHN DOS PASSOS:

On Leave from the Ambulance Corps

R estless and repulsed by small-town values, many American youths cast off convention and left home in the century's second decade. On the east coast, Greenwich Village became a magnet for poets, painters, and writers; in the west the area around Carmel and Monterey formed a strong bohemian community of its own. The most daring seized the Great War as an opportunity to leave the United States altogether. Attracted by the mystique of battle played against a European backdrop were some who would become prominent members of expatriate life in twenties Paris: e. e. cummings, Ernest Hemingway, Malcolm Cowley, Harry Crosby, and John Dos Passos.

It was Dos Passos, in fact, who would write the first significant war novel of his generation, *Three Soldiers*, a work of rage and disillusionment. This and his later novels—in particular the three highly experimental works comprising the *U.S.A.* trilogy—were critically acclaimed and commercially successful, using such innovative and modern techniques as telescoping, the piling up of images, and the lack of transition between scenes to give a cinematic effect.

Dos Passos's background was highly unconventional for the times. His mother, a Maryland socialite, married his father, a prominent lawyer, when Dos Passos was fourteen years old. Much of his youth was spent traveling in Europe, especially in France, giving him a love of adventurous travel that lasted throughout his life.* Writing about Dos Passos years later, Malcolm Cowley would say he was "the greatest traveler in a generation of ambulant writers . . . always on his way to Spain or Russia or Istanbul or the Syrian desert."

After his 1916 graduation from Harvard, where he'd become close friends with e. e. cummings, Dos Passos became a driver with the ambulance corps in France; a year later he transferred to Italy where he served bravely but eventually received a dishonorable discharge for anti-war remarks written in letters home.

Life as an ambulance driver was dangerous and often heartbreaking; those who survived had usually endured the gruesome deaths of friends and comrades. Conditions were filthy, clothes and bedding lice-infested, a bath often unavailable for weeks or even months at a time. Food was scarce and sometimes inedible. In his trench diary of 1918

---

*It also explains why Dos Passos spoke fluent French. Among other expats who did so were Natalie Barney, Ernest Hemingway, Harold Stearns, Janet Flanner, Sylvia Beach, and William Carlos Williams.

Dos Passos wrote of the Corps doctor picking insects from a piece of cheese before popping it in his mouth.

It's easy to imagine the joy the young Dos Passos must have felt on a brief leave in March of 1918. With knapsack on back, he took off on a walking tour of Italy, staying at inns and enjoying regional cuisine. For a while, at least, he could leave the war behind. In a letter to his close friend, Walter Rumsey Marvin, he wrote:

> I don't think . . . that I've ever been in a town so beautiful as Positano. I'm overwhelmed and smothered in beauty—sight and smell and the soft wind off the sea in your ears—Also I have had one of the best dinners ever invented—risotto, omelet, cheese and such oranges as I think the "apples" of the Hesperides must have been—and wine—a light red wine—a wine full of the brisk hills and the great exhilerating space of the sea, and the smell of thyme and gorse and almond blossom and rosemary and basil and lavendar from the fields that make little ribbons of velvet among the shaggy rocks.

*

The Found Meal for John Dos Passos

RISOTTO WITH CLAMS
LEEK FRITTATA
SELECTION OF CHEESES
FRESH ORANGES
LIGHT ITALIAN RED WINE

Risotto with Clams

Risotto with seafood is a specialty on the Italian coast where Dos Passos traveled. Use Italian arborio rice if at all possible—it produces the unique texture that makes a true risotto. If you can't find arborio, try long-grained white rice.

Scrub 2 to 3 dozen small clams under cold water and place in large pot with 1 cup dry white wine. Bring to slow boil, cover, reduce heat slightly and allow to cook until shells have opened. When cool, remove meat from shells, saving cooking wine and juices from clams. Strain liquid through sieve into large saucepan; add 1 cup dry white wine and 4 cups water. Bring to boil, reduce heat to gentle simmer, and cover.

In a heavy, large saucepan, sauté 1 chopped onion and 1 minced garlic clove in 2 tablespoons butter and 2 tablespoons olive oil. When onion has wilted, add 2 tablespoons finely chopped parsley. Continue to cook 1 minute, then add 2 cups arborio rice. Sauté for about a minute; rice should be well coated. Reduce heat until moderate or moderately high (it depends on your stove; when you add liquid, you'll want it to bubble merrily but not furiously). Add 1 cup of the simmering liquid to rice and stir continually until absorbed; be sure to stir around bottom and sides. Add another cup of the liquid, continue to stir. If you run out of liquid near the end, use very hot faucet water. The last time you add liquid, include the clams and 1 teaspoon salt.

This whole procedure will take about 30 minutes. The risotto, when done, should be creamy with a bit of firmness in the rice. Generously grind pepper over the risotto before serving.

Leek Frittata

The "omelet" Dos Passos wrote about was almost certainly a frittata, a dish as popular with the Italians as the traditional omelette is with the French. A frittata is cooked slowly, its filling usually mixed together with the eggs; the result is a concentrated, almost cake-like creation that, unlike an omelet, is delicious hot or cold.

Slice four large, clean leeks into ½-inch rings. Place in ice water and let sit for ½ hour. Drain, rinse carefully, and set aside. Heat 3 tablespoons olive oil in pan large enough to comfortably hold leeks. When oil is hot, add leeks, reduce heat, and continue cooking until soft (approximately 20 minutes). Salt and pepper to taste, remove leeks to bowl and let cool.

Beat 6 eggs (brought to room temperature) in a large bowl; add a pinch of salt and the cooled leeks. Heat 1 tablespoon of oil in large omelet pan; when oil is hot, add leek mixture while agitating pan back and forth. Reduce heat. Allow egg mixture to cook slowly, approximately 10 minutes. When frittata is detached from pan bottom, put plate over pan and turn frittata onto it. Slide frittata back into pan so that reverse side can cook for approximately 4 minutes. Turn onto warm plate and serve.

Selection of Cheeses

Serve Italian cheeses. Think about serving a mild variety such as Taleggio, Bel Paese, or fresh Asiago with a strong cheese such as Gorgonzola or Parmigiano.

Fresh Oranges

Serve the oranges whole, in an attractive bowl. Give each guest a small plate and knife to peel or slice the orange as desired. If possible, serve blood oranges—so juicy and flavorful are they that they could well be the "apples of the Hesperides" to which Dos Passos refers. If blood oranges are unavailable, navel or mandarin oranges are good choices.

Wine Suggestions

Positano, on the mainland close to the island of Capri, is in the Campania wine region, whose best-known red wines are Vesuvio, grown on the volcanic foothills of Mt. Vesuvius, and Gragnano (described by the wine connoisseur Alex Lichine as "so delicious to drink on a flower-laden terrace over the Bay of Naples"). Capri also produces a light red wine called, cleverly enough, Capri. I'd guess that Dos Passos was drinking either the Gragnano or the Capri.

On Leave from the Ambulance Corps

1920

In the United States

Robert McAlmon and William Carlos Williams start *Contact* magazine in Greenwich Village . . . New York Society for the Suppression of Vice launches lawsuit against Margaret Anderson and Jane Heap, publishers of *Little Review*, on obscenity charges stemming from serialization of *Ulysses*; they are convicted and fined $100 . . . Publication of F. Scott Fitzgerald's *This Side of Paradise* . . .

In Paris

Arrivals: Ezra Pound, James Joyce, Bill Bird, Harold Loeb (short stay) . . . Sylvia Beach meets James Joyce . . . Publication of *Pensées d'une Amazone* by Natalie Barney . . .

SYLVIA BEACH AND JAMES JOYCE:

A Literary Encounter

They were a strange duo—a prim preacher's daughter from New Jersey and a half-blind, self-exiled Irish nationalist. But their meeting in 1920, over a cold supper at the home of a mutual friend, would change the scope of modern literature forever. She was Sylvia Beach, proprietor of Shakespeare and Company, the only English-language bookstore on the Left Bank; he was James Joyce, writer.

Beach had come to France in 1916, working as a volunteer farmhand in the Touraine and, later, as a Red Cross secretary in Serbia. In Paris after the war she struck up a friendship with a bookstore owner, Adrienne Monnier, whose Left Bank shop was popular with French writers. Soon Beach decided to open a similar shop for English-language readers, and in November 1919 Shakespeare and Company was born. A year later the bookstore moved to 12, rue de l'Odeon, where it stayed in business until the 1941 German invasion of Paris.

By 1920 Joyce's first novel, *Portrait of the Artist as a Young Man*, had already established him in modernist eyes as the most important writer of the new century; his work in progress, *Ulysses,* was defining him as the most controversial. In the United States, four complete editions of the *Little Review,* which had serialized *Ulysses* since 1918, had been seized and burned by the Post Office for alleged obscenity. In England Harriet Weaver, the gentle Quaker who published five installments of the novel in her literary magazine *Egoist,* hadn't fared much better. Rather than give in to readers' complaints of obscenity by ending the serialization of *Ulysses,* she stopped publishing the magazine altogether. Instead, she said, she would bring *Ulysses* out in book form. So it was that in the summer of 1920 the mild-mannered Joyce found himself in the center of a literary tempest, an unwilling symbol in the fight for artistic freedom.

Few revered him more than Sylvia Beach. In her memoirs she recalled their first meeting, at the home of André Spire, a mutual friend. Beach was so awestruck to be in Joyce's presence, she later wrote, that at first she wanted to run away. But after a cold supper, when Joyce disappeared from the table, she'd calmed down enough to seek him out. She found him shyly secreted between two bookcases. Sylvia introduced herself and finally took a close look at her idol:

He was of medium height, thin, slightly stooped, graceful. One noticed his hands. They were very narrow. On the middle and third fingers of the left hand, he wore rings, the stones in heavy settings. His eyes, a deep blue, with the light of genius in them, were extremely beautiful. I noticed, however, that the right eye had a slightly abnormal look and that the right lens of his glasses was thicker than the left. His hair was thick, sandy-colored, wavy, and brushed back from a high, lined forehead over his tall head. He gave an impression of sensitiveness exceeding any I had ever known. His skin was fair, with a few freckles, and rather flushed. On his chin was a sort of goatee. His nose was well-shaped, his lips narrow and fine-cut. I thought he must have been very handsome as a young man.

The next day, dressed in a dark suit and dirty white sneakers and twirling a cane, Joyce delighted Sylvia by unexpectedly strolling into the bookstore. Thus their friendship began. Sylvia enjoyed Joyce's stiff dignity and elegant, old-fashioned manners; he found her to be knowledgeable about literature and a good listener. Joyce joined Sylvia's lending library that first day, walking off with a play by a fellow Irishman, John Synge.

In September 1920, the New York Society for the Suppression of Vice filed a complaint against Margaret Anderson and Jane Heap, alleging that the July-August *Little Review* contained obscene portions of *Ulysses*. Anderson and Heap were arrested. Brought to trial in February 1921, they were found guilty, fined $50 each, and forbidden to publish excerpts from *Ulysses* in their magazine. At about the same time, Harriet Weaver reluctantly concluded that she would be unable to publish *Ulysses* in England, since no printer would agree to set type for a book by Joyce.

These events slammed the door on Joyce's hopes of seeing *Ulysses* published in English. When he despaired of his prospects to Beach, she immediately offered Shakespeare and Company as a publisher. Joyce accepted without hesitation.

And so, "undeterred by lack of capital, experience, and all the other requisites of a publisher," Beach later wrote, "I went right ahead with *Ulysses*." The next day—April Fool's Day—they made a final, verbal agreement to proceed with one of the century's great literary endeavors.

*

The Found Meal for James Joyce and Sylvia Beach

OYSTERS ON THE HALF SHELL
COLD HAM BRAISED IN MADEIRA WINE
OEUFS EN GELÉE
ASPARAGUS WITH RED-WINE MAYONNAISE
SALADE AIXOISE
SELECTION OF FRENCH CHEESES
BAGUETTES, ROLLS, VARIOUS BREADS
FRUIT IN SEASON

———————

Descriptions of the "delicious cold supper" at which Beach and Joyce met are rather vague, saying only that it consisted of meats, chicken, fish, salad, pastries, and baguettes. The cold supper offered here is typical of the kind of meal that would have been offered that evening at André Spire's home.

Oysters on the Half Shell

The selection of oysters available will depend on where you live. If possible, purchase a wide variety; it's fun to compare and contrast the differing tastes. If you can only find one variety, however, that's fine.

Buy tightly closed oysters, about six per person. If an oyster feels unduly light, it means the occupant is dead; if too heavy, the shell may be full of sand or mud. Once home, scrub the shells thoroughly with a stiff brush. If they won't be used immediately, cover them with damp paper towels and foil, and store them in the refrigerator with the larger, more convex side down so that they will bathe and live in their juices.

To open them you need an oyster knife. Place the oyster on a firm surface, curved side down and with the hinge facing you; poke around the hinge with your finger to find an entry point into which you can insert the knife point. Pry open the hinge. Separate the top shell from the bottom shell containing the oyster, retaining as much juice as possible. Slide a knife beneath the oyster, freeing it from its attachment to the shell, but leave it in place. Arrange oysters on a plate, resting on rock salt or crushed ice. Accompany with lemon quarters or a sauce made from champagne vinegar, minced shallots and cracked black pepper.

Cold Ham Braised in Madeira Wine

Remove rind and fat from a 4- to 5-pound picnic ham, bone out. Place ham in roasting pan to which has been added 2 cups Madeira wine and 3 cups beef stock, fresh or canned. Place ham, uncovered, in preheated 325° oven; let cook for 1½ to 2 hours, basting every 20 minutes with collected juices. When ham is done, lightly dust top and sides with powdered sugar; return to oven and let brown lightly, uncovered, for approximately 10 minutes. Remove ham from oven to platter and allow to cool. Before serving, cut ham into thin slices; arrange meat attractively on platter. Accompany with mustard sauce (page 65).

Oeufs en Gelée

For four eggs, soak 1 tablespoon gelatin in ¼ cup cold water, and then dissolve in ¼ cup boiling canned or home-made chicken stock. Remove pan from stove and add 1¼ cups cold stock, ¼ cups tomato juice, 1½ tablespoons lemon juice, ½ teaspoon salt, ¼ teaspoon paprika. Pour aspic into individual molds so that sides are coated and bottom contains ¼ to ½ inch aspic. Chill until jelled. Place a well-drained, cold poached egg in center of each mold and fill to top with more aspic. Chill. Unmold and arrange on serving platter.

See the chapter on Bricktop, page 163, for the poached egg recipe.

Asparagus with Red-Wine Mayonnaise

Take 2 pounds asparagus, snap off the lower ends, and rinse. Place upright in pan containing ½ inch water, and bring to boil. Cook, covered, until just tender. Drain well, and arrange attractively on platter, surrounding small bowl of Red-Wine Mayonnaise.

Red-Wine Mayonnaise

In a generous-sized bowl, thoroughly beat 2 egg yolks with a whisk. Gradually beat in ½ teaspoon salt, ½ teaspoon lemon juice or tarragon wine vinegar, and—if desired—a dash of finely ground white pepper. Then, drop by drop, beat in 2 cups olive oil. As you add the oil, the mixture will gradually thicken into more than 2 cups of mayonnaise. Reserve half the mayonnaise for future use.

Into the remaining mayonnaise, gradually stir in about ½ cup of dry red wine. Serve with the asparagus.

Salade Aixoise

Prepare dressing by combining in a small mixing bowl: 6 tablespoons high-quality olive oil, 3 tablespoons red wine vinegar, 1 tablespoon capers, 1 teaspoon each finely chopped tarragon and parsley, salt and pepper to taste. Cover and let flavors blend at room temperature for at least an hour before serving.

A Literary Encounter

In a large salad bowl combine 2 cooked, quartered arti-choke hearts; a generous handful of fresh green string beans (lightly cooked and still crisp); 3 medium boiled potatoes cut into bite-sized pieces; 2 medium tomatoes, seeded and chopped; 1 green pepper, seeded and cut into strips; 4 anchovy fillets, rinsed in cold water and chopped into inch-long pieces; ¼ to ½ cup Niçoise olives. Pour dressing over vegetables, toss gently, and serve.

Selection of French Cheeses

For a discussion of French cheeses, see the chapter on Man Ray and Kiki, page 80.

1921

In the United States

First issue of *Broom* (editors: Harold Loeb, Matthew Josephson, Malcolm Cowley, Slater Brown, Alfred Kreymborg) published in New York . . . Josephine Baker appears in *Shuffle Along*, first Broadway musical directed, written, and acted by blacks . . . Publication of *Three Soldiers* by John Dos Passos; *Main Street* by Sinclair Lewis; *America and the Young Intellectual*, edited by Harold Stearns . . .

In Paris

Arrivals: Malcolm Cowley, Ernest Hemingway, Thornton Wilder, Robert McAlmon, Sherwood Anderson, F. Scott and Zelda Fitzgerald (short stay), Man Ray, Berenice Abbott, Marsden Hartley, Djuna Barnes, Gerald and Sara Murphy, Virgil Thomson, Harold Loeb . . . Charlie Chaplin visits for French première of *The Kid*; he is mobbed by hysterical crowds . . . Man Ray begins experiments with rayographs, meets Kiki of Montparnasse . . .

ROBERT MCALMON:
Meeting the In-Laws

The life of Robert McAlmon was an embodiment of the conditional perfect verb tense: he could have been, would have been, should have been—if only one condition or another had been different. That his life didn't turn out the way it should have is one of the tragedies of the Paris years.

Born in Minnesota, McAlmon attended college briefly until 1918, when he joined the fledgling Air Corps. He soon turned his flying experiences into poetry, and in 1919 his first six efforts were published in the influential journal *Poetry*. After a brief stint in Chicago he settled in Greenwich Village—then enjoying its heydey as America's bohemian hub—where he worked for $1 an hour as an artist's model at Cooper Union.* During this period he met, among others, the writers William Carlos Williams and Djuna Barnes, the poet Marianne Moore, and the painter Marsden Hartley.

McAlmon and Williams soon combined energies to publish a short-lived but influential literary journal called

---

*McAlmon was one of the first men in the United States to pose nude.

Contact, whose contributors included Ezra Pound, Kay Boyle, Wallace Stevens, Marianne Moore, and H.D. *Contact* folded when its two editor/publishers ran out of money.

At about the same time, in the early winter of 1921, McAlmon met the English poet Bryher (née Winifred Ellerman), and with lightning speed they married and set sail for Europe. Theirs was an unconsummated marriage of convenience, since McAlmon had as little sexual interest in women as Bryher had in men. With the cover of a husband, Bryher was free to leave her parents' staid London home and live on the continent with her lover, the imagist poet H.D. (Hilda Doolittle). As for McAlmon, the marriage put an end to his hand-to-mouth existence: Bryher's father was one of England's wealthiest citizens, the shipping tycoon Sir John Ellerman.

"It must be remembered," Bryher wrote years later in her memoirs, "that I had been brought up on French rather than English lines and that arranged marriages were perfectly familiar to me. It never occurred to me at the time that there was anything irregular." McAlmon was equally comfortable with the situation. Writing to Williams from Paris, he emphasized that the marriage was a mutual agreement, legal rather than romantic.

After a short stay in London, where McAlmon was warmly received into the unsuspecting Ellerman family, he and Bryher traveled to the continent and went their separate ways—she to Italy and H.D., he to Paris and literary destiny.

From the moment he arrived in Paris everything about the young McAlmon augured success: a writer of acknowledged promise, he was also charming, intelligent, witty—and now rich, since he received a stipend from Bryher's father. He made friends easily, eventually counting among them James Joyce, Nancy Cunard, Man Ray, Djuna Barnes, Jean Cocteau, Marcel Duchamp, Nina Hamnett, Harold Loeb, Ezra Pound, Kay Boyle, Constantin Brancusi, and, until he fought bitterly with them, Ernest Hemingway and Gertrude Stein. Years later Sylvia Beach remembered McAlmon as the most popular man on the Left Bank, so well liked that whenever he switched allegiance from one café to another so did most of the English-speaking expat crowd.

McAlmon soon formed a publishing venture, the now-legendary Contact Editions. Between 1922 and 1931, the official year of its demise, Contact published twenty-two books, the quality of which assure McAlmon a firm place in American literary history. Among Contact's publications were the first book by Ernest Hemingway, *Three Stories and Ten Poems*; Gertrude Stein's *The Making of Americans*; *The Ladies Almanack* by Djuna Barnes; the *Contact Collection of Contemporary Writers*, which included works by Joyce, Pound, Ford, Barnes, Stein, and Hemingway; and six books of his own, including the critically well received *A Hasty Bunch* and *Post-Adolescence*. Most of Contact's books were printed in a limited edition of three hundred and are extremely valuable today.

McAlmon was an easy touch, often making outright

gifts of cash to tide friends over rough times. James Joyce, whom he revered, received a monthly stipend of $150. For the poet Emanuel Carnevali, impoverished and ill with encephalitis, he paid a year's care in a private sanatorium. He apparently gave some financial aid to Djuna Barnes, and his generosity to Kay Boyle through trying times is legendary.

Slowly, however, McAlmon's golden-boy quality lost its luster. Bitter at his lack of success as a writer, he lashed out at others, frequently disparaging his more successful friends.* In a letter to his editor, Maxwell Perkins, Scott Fitzgerald wrote:

> McAlmon is a bitter rat and I'm not surprised at anything he does or says. He's failed as a writer and tries to fortify himself by tying up to the big boys like Joyce and Stein and despising everything else. Part of his quarrel with Ernest [Hemingway] some years ago was because he assured Ernest that I was a fairy—God knows he shows more creative imagination in his malice than in his work. Next he told Callaghan that Ernest was a fairy. He's a pretty good person to avoid.

---

*McAlmon received a fair share of critical praise, but the consensus among writers was that he needed to spend time revising and editing. This he refused to do, believing the original flash of inspiration should stand as written, and his work suffered in the process. Flashes of brilliance were often lost in sloppy, meandering prose. A popular ditty of the day went: "I'd rather live in Oregon/and pack salmon/Than live in Nice/and write like Robert McAlmon."

McAlmon's drinking—always a topic of gossip—became scandalous. "The drinks were often on him, and, alas! often in him," mourned Sylvia Beach. Alice Toklas recalled that "it was of McAlmon that Hemingway once said, I do not like to see him throw up my royalties." The stories from this period abound: he screamed profane names at friends in public, peppered nightclub audiences with obscenities, whirled atop café tables while boasting of his bisexuality. On at least one occasion the nightclub owner Bricktop slipped him a mickey finn to stop him from fighting with her customers.

McAlmon's life became a vicious circle. The more he drank, the less he wrote; the less he wrote, the smaller his chances for recognition and success; the less recognition he won, the more bitter he became; the more bitter, the more he drank. John Glassco, recalling an evening on the town with McAlmon in the late twenties, wrote: "McAlmon's own capacity for alcohol was astounding: within the next half-hour he drank half a dozen double whiskies with no apparent effect. His conversation, consisting of disjointed expletives and explosions of scorn, was fascinating in its anarchy . . . all people were fools or snobs. He spoke of his friends with utter contempt."

His contempt for everyone and everything increased. In his memoirs of the Paris years, *Being Geniuses Together*,* he had scarcely a kind word for anyone (he partic-

---

*Long after McAlmon's death, Kay Boyle revised the text of *Being Geniuses Together* and added supplementary chapters of her own. The expanded version was published in 1968.

Meeting the In-Laws

ularly excoriates Hemingway, Stein, and T. S. Eliot). By the end of the twenties, McAlmon had few friends left. When he finally returned to the United States in the thirties, he fell into obscurity. He would die, largely unmourned, in 1956.

One of the few truly happy moments in *Being Geniuses Together* was McAlmon's description of the first meeting in London with his in-laws, when Paris and all that was to come still lay in the future:

Her Ladyship met Bryher and me at Victoria Station and all was sweetness and charm and love, for now I was her dear boy, one of the children. That was all right with me, because I was and am decidedly fond of her Ladyship. A nice dinner was awaiting us. . . . There was caviar served with sweet pancakes over which heavy cream was poured. There followed fresh salmon with a rich sauce, and partridge, and then apple or raspberry pie, also to be served with cream. It was a meal to dream about.

*

The Found Meal for Robert McAlmon and Bryher

CAVIAR WITH BLINIS AND CREAM
FRESH SALMON STEAKS IN CREAM
ROAST PARTRIDGE
RASPBERRY PIE WITH CREAM

Blinis and Cream

Many Parisian restaurants of the 1920s were owned by Russian emigrants. One of the most popular was the Ermitage Russe at 21 Boissy d'Anglais, a short distance from Jean Cocteau's nightclub, Le Boeuf sur le Toit. A popular dish on the Ermitage menu was blinis and cream, doubtless similar to the caviar and pancakes McAlmon mentioned.

Dissolve ½ envelope (½ tablespoon) dry yeast in 1½ cups lukewarm milk. Make a sponge consisting of ½ cup white flour and ½ cup buckwheat flour, ½ teaspoon salt, 2 teaspoons of sugar, the yeast mixture, and 3 egg yolks. Let rise in warm place until double in bulk, about 1 hour. Mix ½ cup each white flour and buckwheat flour; add to sponge mixture along with another 1½ cups milk, forming a smooth batter with consistency of heavy cream. Allow this mixture to rise until double in bulk, about 1 hour. Beat 3 egg whites into soft peaks and fold into doubled batter. Cook blinis on a hot buttered griddle for a ½ minute or so on each side. Keep warm.

Blinis should be delicate and thin. To serve, make a stack of 2 or 3 3-inch blinis, each brushed with a little melted butter. Top with as much black caviar as your budget can afford and a double teaspoon of Russian smetana (similar to but thinner and more flavorful than sour cream; you can make your own by mixing 1 pint of heavy cream with 1 teaspoon of sour cream and allowing the blend to sit out in a warm place overnight. Whip just before serving).

For more information about purchasing caviar, see page 198 in the chapter on Harry and Caresse Crosby.

Fresh Salmon Steaks in Cream

This dish is based on a traditional English recipe for salmon.

Dice and sauté 2 or 3 shallots in a little butter. Place 4 salmon steaks in a shallow covered casserole. Add the shallots, ½ cup of heavy cream, salt, and freshly ground black pepper. Cover and bake in a 350° oven for 12 minutes. Remove the salmon to a platter, dress it with the cream and garnish with lemon slices and parsley.

Roast Partridge

In the United States the term *partridge* is a catchall word encompassing ruffed grouse, quail, and sometimes pheasant.

Clean 4 grouse or 8 quail, brushing generously inside and out with a mixture of brandy and lemon juice. Rub the birds with butter, salt and pepper them, and then lard with pork fat, securing the fat with a string. Place birds in uncovered roasting pan breast side down and put in preheated 425° oven, reducing heat immediately to 350°. Allow 20 to 25 minutes per pound cooking time. Turn the birds after about a third of the cooking time has passed; baste regularly with accumulated fat in the pan. About 10 minutes before the birds are done, remove larding fat and allow them to brown. Let birds rest in a warm place for 5 minutes, then arrange on serving platter; spoon pan juices over them. Garnish platter with watercress.

Raspberry Pie with Cream

Work together ⅓ cup shortening and 1 tablespoon chilled butter. With a pastry blender or fork, work half the mixture into 1 cup sifted white flour and ½ teaspoon salt. When blended, cut in the remaining half of shortening, working until dough is crumbly and pea-sized. Sprinkle with 2 tablespoons cold water and work dough with your hands. When dough can be gathered into a ball, it's ready (you may have to add a bit more water before it reaches this point). Cover with waxed paper and refrigerate for 1 hour, and then roll out. Line a 9-inch lightly buttered pie pan with pastry, creating fluted edge. Roll leftover pieces into a ball and roll out again; cut into strips to be used as lattice on pie.

Clean 4 cups raspberries and combine in a bowl with ½ cup sugar, 2 tablespoons arrowroot, and 2 tablespoons fresh lemon juice. Mix gently and let rest 10 minutes. Transfer berries to pie shell. Weave lattice pieces in crisscross fashion across pie top. Place pie in preheated 350° oven and bake for 35 to 45 minutes, until crust is golden. Serve warm with jug of fresh cream.

A Tea Party

The painter Nina Hamnett was a true Montparnasse star, glittering hot and bright at the center of the Left Bank universe. Her affairs and friendships ran the gamut of the day's well-known artists, many of whom painted, sculpted, or wrote about her. James Joyce said she was one of the most vital women he'd ever met. Jimmy the Barman called her the stage director of the Dingo and the Dôme. Robert McAlmon reveled in her ready wit, in her knowledge of everybody and everything, and most especially in the fact that she never let truth get in the way of a good story.

With boundless energy, Hamnett was everywhere, doing it all: in the afternoon she might play the guitar and sing for André Gide; that evening she would share a piano bench with Rudolph Valentino, interrupting their melodic duos to introduce him to James Joyce; later that night she would very likely put on a hand-me-down, jewel-encrusted ball gown and take off nightclubbing on the arm of a count. Being "inordinately vain and proud of my figure," she often removed her clothes and danced naked at parties. She loved to recite poems and sing in cafés, often accompanying herself on guitar, though her taste—which ran to titles popular with sailors like "The Servant Girl in Drury Lane" and "She Was Poor But She Was Honest"—wasn't always appreciated by the faint-hearted.

Then there were the trips to Brittany, and Céret, and Collioure, always with a new *Grand Amour,* usually another painter. There were the evenings of wandering the streets dressed like a male gangster. There were the endless parties at Countess Something's or Prince Whatsit's, and the nights—most of them, in fact—at Le Boeuf sur le Toit, the in-est of the in nightclubs. Hamnett's autobiography is crammed to the end-pages with late hours: "We then went to Les Halles and had supper or breakfast or both, and some white wine, and returned to Montparnasse about eight A.M." "We got [home] to Montparnasse about nine A.M." "I arrived home about two-thirty, feeling very much pleased with life and with myself." "Finally went home about five-thirty A.M." And it goes on.

The thing most startling about Nina Hamnett is that, despite a life of wild adventure and nights of ferocious drinking, she was a quite good painter who produced prolifically through these years. *Il faut travailler,* she insisted, and work she did. The daughter of an English army officer, Hamnett had a conventional background from which she broke away as soon as possible. She studied at the London School of Art and worked briefly at Roger Fry's Omega Workshop, then producing innovative fabrics with cubist designs. A short visit to Paris in 1912, when she was twenty-two, convinced her she should live there and soon she did.

Before long she counted among her friends the artistic glitterati and royal nabobs of the day. It's doubtful that anyone in Paris had such a varied collection of friends: Amedeo Modigliani (whose studio she took over after his death), Man Ray, Guillaume Apollinaire, Lady Asquith, Constantin Brancusi, Kiki, Nancy Cunard, Ronald Firbank, James Joyce, Fernand Léger, Princess Murat, Robert McAlmon, Kay Boyle, Francis Picabia, Arthur Rubenstein, the Sitwells. Hamnett became particularly close friends with Jean Cocteau, the young French poet, painter, and cinéaste. Addicted to opium, Cocteau was a great social butterfly, celebrated for his brilliance, elegance, and rather cruel wit. This excerpt from *Laughing Torso*, Hamnett's breathless and ceaselessly entertaining autobiography, recounts the time she brought Osbert Sitwell to Cocteau's:

> [The composer] Willie Walton was also in Paris, and we all dined together that evening. Osbert said that he would like me to meet a friend of his, Sir Coleridge Kennard, who would like to meet Cocteau and Radiguet. Sir Coleridge had a Rolls-Royce, and Osbert said that if I arranged a day they would come to the studio and fetch me. I put on my best clothes and waited, hoping to impress the neighbours, and especially my concièrge. I waited behind the front door, but to my bitter disappointment they came in an old and very shaky taxi. We went to the Rue d'An-

jou, the house of Madame Cocteau, Jean's Mother, where he had some rooms to himself. We were shown into a very large room which was filled with all kinds of amusing and wonderful things. On the wall was a portrait of him by Marie Laurencin. A bust of Radiguet, by Jacques Lipschitz, which was very good. A portrait of Cocteau by Jacques Emile Blanche, one by Derain, drawings of Picasso, a glass ship in a case, and on the wall by the fireplace, a most wonderful photograph of Arthur Rimbaud, looking like an angel, that I had never seen before. Cocteau went to a cupboard that was filled with drawers and, out of each drawer, produced a drawing or a painting of himself by, I think, nearly every celebrated artist in France. We had tea and everyone talked a great deal.

✳

The Found Meal for Nina Hamnett and Jean Cocteau

FORMOSA OOLONG TEA

Formosa Oolong Tea

> Neither a green nor black tea, oolong is something in between. Many experts consider the smoky Formosa oolong to be the very best tea available—exactly what you'd expect Cocteau to offer his guests.

Bring a generous amount of very pure water to boil. Heat teapot by rinsing with boiling water. Put 1 teaspoonful of Formosa oolong or other tea into pot for each person; add an extra spoonful "for the pot." Add boiling water, approximately 1 cup per teaspoon of tea. Stir well. Let steep for 5 minutes. Serve.

Suggested Accompaniments

Try small crustless tea sandwiches such as those mentioned by Kay Boyle in her novel *My Next Bride*. In this book, which takes place in Paris during the twenties, two characters meet at Rumplemeyer's—a favorite eating spot among Americans. There they enthuse over the restaurant's nut/mayonnaise and olive/cheese sandwiches.

1922

In the United States

Isadora Duncan banned from Boston stage for wearing see-through dress while praising Soviets; unclear whether dress or praise precipitated banning . . . U.S. Post Office burns 500 copies of James Joyce's recently published novel, *Ulysses* . . . Publication of *Babbit* by Sinclair Lewis; *The Beautiful and Damned* by F. Scott Fitzgerald; *The Enormous Room* by e. e. cummings; *Civilization in the United States*, edited by Harold Stearns . . .

In Paris

First publication in book form of *Ulysses* (Shakespeare and Company) . . . Arrivals: Ford Madox Ford, Harry and Caresse Crosby, Janet Flanner, Solita Solano; Kay Boyle comes to France, though not to Paris . . . Robert McAlmon founds Contact Editions . . .

ERNEST HEMINGWAY I:

The Hunger

I magine that you are Ernest Hemingway, a tall, burly, good-looking young man with a slow, easy grin. You look more like a football player than a writer, but it's a writer that you want to be. Although you never went to college, you wrote well enough for your high-school paper and literary magazine to land a reporter's job on the *Kansas City Star*. You liked it there all right, but you were only eighteen and you knew there had to be more to life than Kansas City. So you went off to Europe and the war, driving an ambulance for the Red Cross and distinguishing yourself as the first American wounded in Italy. Your knee was shot up pretty bad and you spent a few months in a Milan hospital where you fell in love with a beautiful nurse named Agnes. Then you came home to Oak Park, Illinois, strutted around for a while in your uniform, and finally took another reporter's job with the *Toronto Star*.

On a trip to Chicago you met a lovely woman named Hadley Richardson and in a short time the two of you married. The famous writer Sherwood Anderson, whom you had met through a friend, invited you and your wife to dinner one night. Anderson, just returned from Paris, knew how much you wanted to write. He also knew how difficult it was to find the time to write when holding a job. He told you to go live in Paris if you really want to be a writer. It's cheap, he said, and that's where you'll find the great writers experimenting with the English language, people like Gertrude Stein, Ezra Pound, James Joyce.

Your wife thinks this is a wonderful idea. She has a small yearly income from a trust fund, and that, combined with the extra money you would earn as a part-time correspondent for the *Toronto Star*, would be enough to live on. Most of your days would be free for writing.

You step off the train in Paris in late December 1921; you are only a year older than the century. You quickly find an apartment; it's tiny, without plumbing, above a *bal musette* whose nightly accordian music often keeps you awake—but it's cheap. You find an even cheaper room where you can go to write, for you need to be alone to write. You've written before, of course; you've been a newspaper reporter, after all, and you've fooled around a bit with fiction and poetry. But now you are *really* trying to write for the first time, trying in a way that is clean, clear, and honest. You're scared, because you don't know if you can do it. But when you get scared, you say to yourself: "All you have to do is write one true sentence. Write the truest sentence that you know." And eventually you do write a true sentence. But the work is hard and slow and you wonder if you are any good.

You don't spend all your time in that lonely room, of

course. You like to wander the streets, and you quickly pick up the Parisian slang. You go to the cafés sometimes, but not too often; you'll soon develop a contempt for the dilettante café-sitters, those who call themselves artists but spend their working hours sleeping off the previous night's excess. You make a deal with the *Toronto Star* to write thirty articles by March, which gets you out and about playing the journalist. You and your wife travel to Switzerland for two weeks. You begin to find partners for tennis, boxing, or going to the bicycle races.

Then there are the letters of introduction given to you by Anderson. You want to use them, but you're so shy that you hesitate. You never *do* use one of them, the one for Sylvia Beach at Shakespeare and Company. Instead you just walk through her door one day and hang awkwardly about until, curious, she asks you questions about yourself.

Beach likes you, and years later will say that she considered you a well-educated young man, one who knew the history and politics of many countries, who spoke several languages, and who had learned it all himself rather than in universities. She finds you far more mature than the other young writers on the Left Bank. "In spite of a certain boyishness," she confided in her memoirs, "he was exceptionally wise and self-reliant . . . serious and competent in whatever he did." You would one day write the truest sentence ever put to print about Beach: "No one that I ever knew was nicer to me."

But Beach, of course, *sells* books, doesn't write them; it's the recipients of the other two letters—both writers—that you've been reluctant to meet. They are famous and you are a nobody, quite unsure of yourself though you show the world a cocky exterior. You decide to tackle the less frightening writer, Ezra Pound, in February. At first you can't stand him, dressed as he is like a bohemian out of a bad Whistler fantasy, but soon enough you form a friendship. Pound takes a strong liking to you and begins to promote your writing and your name; you, in turn, teach him to box.

It isn't until sometime in March that you gather the courage to use your third letter of introduction, the one addressed to the most famous American writer living in Paris, Gertrude Stein. You've heard a lot about her, as has anyone interested seriously in modern fiction or art: she's a forty-eight-year-old legend who has not only shared in the birth of modernism but been the friend of the greatest artists of the century. And you? You're a young guy who wants to write, that's all, and you haven't yet done much work that's any good.

But Stein develops an interest in you right from the start. She later describes you as "extraordinarily good-looking," and is pleased with the way you sit before her attentively listening and looking. Her friend Miss Toklas is not too crazy about you and never will be, but of course she is polite. You and your wife love the big studio with its paintings, like a fine room in the world's best museum—except there's a fireplace, and it's warm and cozy, and they give you wonderful things to eat and liqueurs made from purple plums and wild raspberries. Yes, you like Miss Stein a lot, although you think Miss Toklas is frightening.

The friendship with Stein will grow by leaps and bounds, developing into that of master/disciple, and for a few years the relationship will be mutually beneficial, providing you both a literary boost and warm companionship. When you begin to work on Ford Madox Ford's *Transatlantic Review* you will see to it that Stein's *chef d'oeuvre*, *The Making of Americans*, is serialized. In turn she will teach you quite a lot about writing, about the nature of words and their rhythms, and about the uses of repetition. These lessons will combine well with Pound's belief in absolute simplicity, and with your newspaperman's proclivity for clean prose. Your style will begin to emerge.

In the future will be the first book, *Three Stories and Ten Poems*, published by Robert McAlmon's Contact Editions; and short on its heels the second book, *In Our Time*, published by Bill Bird's Three Mountains Press. Though very small editions, they will be well reviewed, as will be the poems and short stories in magazines. Increasingly you will be talked about, admired, envied. The break will come with Gertrude Stein, but by that time you will not need her any more. You will have published your first novel, *The Sun Also Rises*, and already they will be saying that you are the best writer of your generation.

But that's all in the future, and it's still your first years in Paris and you're writing every morning in the tiny rented room. The winters are exceptionally cold, and sometimes you go to write in a warm café on Place St. Michel. By now you've given up journalism completely, working only on your fiction. You are very discouraged, because nobody is buying your stories and you wonder sometimes if it's because they're no good. You are often hungry because there just isn't enough money now, and there are times when you eat no lunch. One day instead of eating you try to walk off your hunger in the icy streets and when that doesn't work decide to occupy your mind with a visit to Sylvia Beach. She has mail for you: a German newspaper has used something you wrote and has sent you 600 francs.

You take the money and walk quickly to Lipp's, where you order a liter of beer, potato salad, and a sausage. So happy does this simple meal make you that, when you're an old man, you will still remember it. You will write about it like this:

> The beer was very cold and wonderful to drink. The pommes à l'huile were firm and marinated and the olive oil delicious. I ground black pepper over the potatoes and moistened the bread in the olive oil. After the first heavy draft of beer I drank and ate very slowly. When the pommes à l'huile were gone I ordered another serving and a cervelas. This was a sausage like a heavy, wide frankfurter split in two and covered with a special mustard sauce.
>
> I mopped up all the oil and all of the sauce with bread and drank the beer slowly until it began to lose its coldness . . .

When you are through, you lean back and think about your writing. Perhaps because you are no longer hungry, you feel sure that the stories are good and that you should continue on. If you remain strong, you think, someday people will understand. Someday they will want to read your stories. "It only takes time," you think, "and it only needs confidence."

✶

The Found Meal for Ernest Hemingway

CERVELAS WITH MUSTARD SAUCE
POMMES DE TERRE À L'HUILE
BEER

Cervelas with Mustard Sauce

> Cervelas are fat, short sausages made of pork meat, usually seasoned with garlic. If you have trouble finding cervelas, substitute any high-quality pork or pork/garlic sausage.

Plunge 4 fresh cervelas or other pork/garlic sausages into a pot of boiling water, reduce heat, and let simmer for 5 minutes. Remove and rinse with cold water. In frying pan, melt small amount butter over moderate heat. Add sausages and cook until lightly browned. Serve with Mustard Sauce.

Mustard Sauce

In a small mixing bowl combine 2 tablespoons Dijon-style mustard and 3 tablespoons boiling water. Slowly add, drop by drop, ⅓ cup olive oil, beating constantly with a wire whip. The resulting sauce should be creamy. Add salt and pepper to taste, lemon juice if desired.

Pommes de Terre à l'Huile

Wash and peel 2 pounds boiling potatoes and drop into a pan of boiling, salted water. Cover and let boil for 30 minutes or until potatoes are tender when pierced with a thin knife. Drain. Cut into ⅛-inch-thick slices as soon as you can handle them without burning your fingers, placing slices into large bowl. Mix together 4 tablespoons dry white wine and 3 tablespoons fresh or canned beef broth, pouring mixture over warm potatoes. Toss gently.

In a separate bowl, beat together 2 tablespoons red wine vinegar, 1 teaspoon Dijon-type mustard, ½ teaspoon salt; gradually beat in 6 tablespoons olive oil a few drops at a time. Add 3 tablespoons minced shallots. Adjust seasonings. Pour dressing over potatoes and toss gently. Serve.

A Few Words About French Beer

The ancient Gauls drank a barley-flavored beer, and to this day the majority of French beers are made from barley. French beer tends to be light, with a crisp aftertaste, though some regions of France produce a dark, heavy beer. Good French beers include Kronenbourg, La Belle Strasbourgeoise, Brasseurs Biere de Paris, Brassins de Garde Saint Leonard, "33" Export, and "33" Extra Dry.

JAMES JOYCE:

A Gentile Collation

I t's hard to imagine now the furor that greeted publication of James Joyce's *Ulysses* in 1922. The reactions, both pro and con, bring to mind a sort of religious hysteria:

Senator Reed Smoot of Utah, on the floor of the U.S. Senate, said that his ten minutes' skimming of the book was "enough to indicate that it is written by a man with a diseased mind and soul so black that he would even obscure the darkness of Hell."

Janet Flanner recalled that "the publication in toto of *Ulysses* in 1922 was indubitably the most exciting, important, historic single literary event of the early Paris expatriate literary colony . . . In its unique qualities, in 1922 it burst over us, young in Paris, like an explosion in print whose words and phrases fell upon us like a gift of tongues, like a less than holy Pentecostal experience."

Malcolm Cowley, then a young writer living in Paris, later wrote: "The paramount hero of the new age was Joyce, and his *Ulysses* came to be revered by the new writers almost as the Bible was by Primitive Methodists."

Joyce, born near Dublin in 1882, was the oldest of ten

children in an impoverished family. He managed none-theless to graduate from Dublin's University College, where he studied Norwegian so he could read Ibsen in the original. After graduation he went to Paris to study medi-cine, but soon devoted himself to writing. On a return trip to Ireland he met and married Nora Barnacle. Soon there-after, in 1904, they moved to Switzerland; Joyce taught at the Berlitz school and over the next ten years wrote, among other things, *Dubliners* and *A Portrait of the Artist as a Young Man*. Both books received wide critical praise.

Meanwhile, Joyce began *Ulysses*, a work originally con-ceived as a tale for *Dubliners*. *Ulysses*, which would take seven years to complete, was a big, sprawling, bawdy evo-cation of lower-middle-class Dublin life, told mainly through the shifting consciousness of three people. Like another genius of English literature, Shakespeare, Joyce felt confined by current language, so he frequently in-vented his own. He defied traditional strictures, using, for instance, many narrative voices that come and go with out identification. Joyce enters his characters' minds, en-abling the reader to becomes involved in stream-of-con-sciousness thought. Experiences previously considered out of literary bounds—sex, urination, fetal develop-ment—are brought into the open. In short, *Ulysses* broke, tilled, sowed, and reaped new ground, changing the scope of English literature in this century.

By the time *Ulysses* was published by Sylvia Beach in 1922, Joyce's eyes were so damaged by glaucoma that he found both reading and writing difficult. He often wore an eye patch, and almost always wore sunglasses. Though gentle and mild mannered, Joyce was no saint; he liked to drink and frequently went carousing with friends. Often carried home unconscious, he'd invariably be taken in hand at the door by the complaining but ever-forgiving Nora.

Joyce was of medium height, thin and graceful with long, narrow hands. On two fingers of his left hand he wore heavy rings with stones. He usually carried a cane, which he twirled as he walked, and he liked to wear tennis shoes. He didn't care much about food, but loved to entertain, usually inviting people to his favorite restaurant, Trianons, where he insisted they order anything they liked. He almost always drank white wine; he wasn't fussy about its quality. He frequently sang Irish love songs or Italian opera; he had a trained tenor voice, which was reputedly quite beautiful. Most people were intimidated when meeting him; it wasn't only that he was famous, but that his shy reserve left people grasping for conversational straws.

Joyce often became abstracted; a single word uttered by someone could cause his mind to leap away from the conversation. The American painter George Biddle, writing in his memoirs, *An American Artist's Story*, recalled meeting Joyce for the first time. He felt that Joyce "was so aggressively silent and achieved such an opaque front that I was beginning to count my evening as wasted." However, after a second bottle of Chablis, Joyce livened up. When someone asked what he thought of the latest book by Sherwood Anderson, he replied matter-of-factly that he hadn't read *belles lettres* for over ten years. Everyone present exchanged shocked glances: James Joyce, the genius of modern letters, doesn't read literature? According to Biddle, when Joyce was asked what he *did* read, he replied:

> "Oh, farmers' almanacs, fishing guides, hotel circulars, catalogues of department stores and mail-order houses, dictionaries of modern slang, and of course the advertisements in your American quality magazines."
>
> He was not interested in contemporary literature, or yet in life. Like some ardent geologist, with hammer and receptacle, knocking his way over the earth's crust, collecting pretty pebbles, garnets, semiprecious stones, he, essentially the poet, the mouther of words, was ever searching, in almanacs or sport catalogues, for some new, earthy, glowing bit of imagery.

But Joyce was by no means an alienated social being, and the main reason for this was Nora. The frequent evocations of Nora in memoirs of the time discuss her robust health, earthy Irish humor, and acceptance of James's foibles. Most people describe her as extraordinarily pretty, with red curly hair and a strong Irish inflection in her voice. She was not an intellectual, and made no secret of the fact that she'd barely read a thing authored by her husband; she claimed she just couldn't make heads or tails of his writing. She finally read Molly Bloom's *Ulysses* soliloquy after hearing so much about it. "I guess the man's a

A Gentile Collation

genius," she reported to Robert McAlmon, "but what a dirty mind he has, hasn't he?"

Here's an example of Joyce's wordplay from *Ulysses*:

How did Bloom prepare a collation for a gentile?

He poured into two teacups two level spoonfuls, four in all, of Epps's soluble cocoa and proceeded according to the directions for use printed on the label, to each adding after sufficient time for infusion the prescribed ingredients for difficusion in the manner and in the quantity prescribed.

What supererogatory marks of special hospitality did the host show his guest?

Relinquishing his symposiarchal right to the moustache cup of imitation Crown Derby presented to him by his only daughter, Millicent (Milly), he substituted a cup identical with that of his guest and served extraordinarily to his guest and, in reduced measure, to himself the viscous cream ordinarily reserved for the breakfast of his wife Marion (Molly).

Was the guest conscious of and did he acknowledge these marks of hospitality?

His attention was directed to them by his host jocosely, and he accepted them seriously as they drank in jocoserious silence Epps's massproduct, the creature cocoa.

*

COCOA

Cocoa

In a saucepan over very low heat combine 1 cup boiling water, ¼ cup of your favorite powdered cocoa, a dash of salt, and sugar to taste (approximately 3 tablespoons). Mix thoroughly. Add 3 cups scalded milk. Stir gently while mixture slowly heats, approximately 3 minutes. If desired, add 1 teaspoon vanilla near the end. Remove from heat, beat lightly with wire whisk, and pour into moustache cups or mugs.

1923

In the United States

Broadway premiere of *The Adding Machine* by Elmer Rice
... Publication of *A Book* by Djuna Barnes ...

In Paris

Dada completes transition into Surrealism ... Première
of Man Ray's surrealist film, *Return to Reason* ... The
Jockey, a nightclub with cowboy motif, opens in Montpar-
nasse; it's an immediate smash ... Première of Stravinsky's ballet *Les Noces* by Ballets Russe ... Gerald Murphy's
Razor creates stir at Salon des Indépendants ... Arrivals:
George Antheil, Margaret Anderson, Jane Heap ... Composition of Violin Sonata No. 1 by George Antheil ...
Paris Publication of Ernest Hemingway's first book, *Three
Stories and Ten Poems* (Contact Editions); *Indiscretions* by
Ezra Pound (Three Mountains Press) ... The Rotonde
forbids women to smoke or appear hatless on terrace,
causing boycott by English-speaking Quarterites who
start drinking across the street at the Dôme; Malcolm
Cowley arrested for punching Rotonde owner ...

KIKI AND MAN RAY:
Kiki Cooks

I t was a clear case of love at first sight. He was an American, new to Paris, virtually penniless; she was a transplanted Burgundian, an artist's model and cabaret singer of bawdy songs. He spoke little French and she possessed not a word of English, but when he saw her across a crowded café, he arranged an introduction on the spot. That evening they went to the movies where he held her hand, and afterward he asked her to pose. She undressed and he took a few photos, but soon grew distracted by desire. "Other thoughts surged in," he later wrote. "I told her to dress and we went out to the café."

The next day he showed her the prints, which pleased her so much that she went behind a screen and removed all her clothes. When she reappeared, she sat beside him. Man Ray recalled discreetly that he took no pictures that afternoon. Typically, Alice Prin—commonly called Kiki— was more straightforward: "Now," she wrote, "he's my lover." She moved into his studio and stayed six years.

Man Ray was a fairly conventional self-taught painter living in Greenwich Village when he visited the Armory Show in 1913 and came face to face with modern art for the first time. Excited by what he saw, he began experimenting with his own work. Two years later he met Marcel Duchamp,* who was visiting New York, and the two became friends. Introduced by Duchamp to Dadaist theories, Ray produced machine-like works in protest against industrial encroachment into everyday life. He soon found himself at the center of the American Dada movement.

Invited to Paris by Duchamp, Ray arrived on July 22, 1921. He was already well known among Dada's founders—André Breton, Louis Aragon, Jacques Rigaut, Tristan Tzara, and Philippe Soupault—who welcomed him at dinner the night he arrived. Soon he was an integral member of their group.

Ray—the best-known American artist in Paris between the wars—thrived creatively in his new home, constantly breaking new ground. As a painter, he was one of the first to explore the surreal dimensions of the mind. His Rayograms—photographs made without use of a camera—turned the everyday object into something startling, clearly epitomizing Dada concepts.‡ As a filmmaker he introduced ideas and technical innovations that shocked

---

*Duchamp's *Nude Descending a Staircase* had been the Armory Show's most controversial work.

‡A Rayogram of the mid-1920s was auctioned for $126,000 in October 1990, setting a record price for a single photograph. The record was later broken by Soviet photographer Alexander Rodchenko ($181,000), but seized again by Ray in 1993 when his 1930 photograph, "Glass Tears," was auctioned by Sotheby's for $190,000.

many: the première of his film *The Return to Reason* caused riots. With photos such as *Le Violon d'Ingres*—in which he superimposed a violin's soundholes on Kiki's back, thus turning her into a human musical instrument—he broadened the scope of photography. As the unofficial court photographer of the Left Bank, his portraits of artists and writers delve far below the surface, revealing secrets of character. Among his greatest works are thousands of photographs of Kiki, which capture her every mood, gesture, guise.

Kiki, born in Burgundy to an impoverished mother and a nameless father, ran away to Paris at the age of thirteen. She drifted for a time into the *demi-monde* of prostitution, pimps, and drug addicts, eventually finding work as an artist's model. A warm nature and roguish humor made Kiki popular with artists and models alike, and soon she was thriving at the center of Left Bank life. By the time of her 1921 meeting with Ray she was considered the queen of Montparnasse, with a table on permanent reserve at the Dôme.

But greater things lay ahead. Kiki painted, primitive and colorful works which few took seriously until her first sellout show in 1927. Her 1929 memoirs, *The Education of a French Model*, were banned for obscenity in the United States, but sold well in France and are now a valuable collector's item. Ernest Hemingway wrote the introduction, a two-edged sword if there ever was one: ". . . you have a book here written by a woman who was never a lady at any time. For about ten years she was about as close as people get nowadays to being a Queen, but that, of course, is very different from being a lady."

Kiki never pretended to be a lady, and her memoirs make that clear. It's all there: some of the less savory things she was forced to do to earn money while barely in her teens; the exploitive love affairs; her arrest for prostitution; frank descriptions of her lovers' physical endowments; and many nude photos.

Above all, Kiki is remembered for her artistic collaboration with Man Ray, a collaboration in which he was always the creator, she the ever-changing medium. There were, first of all, the thousands of photographs. And the 1928 movie, *Étoile de Mer*, in which she starred. Perhaps strangest of all was Ray's use of Kiki's face as a canvas on which to create temporary works of art. Kay Boyle recalled the results:

> Man Ray had designed Kiki's face for her, and painted it on with his own hand. He would begin by shaving her eyebrows off . . . and then putting other eyebrows back, in any color he might have selected for her mask that day, sometimes as fine as thread and sometimes as thick as your finger, and at any angle he chose. Her heavy eyelids might be done in copper one day and in royal blue another, or else in silver or jade. . . . Tonight they were opaline. She was heavy-featured and voluptuous, her voice as hoarse as that of a vegetable hawker, her hair smooth as a crow's glistening wing.

Other descriptions recall her dead-white face, beauty marks that shifted in both location and color, spit-curls, green feline eyes, and Rubenesque body.

Despite their reputation as eccentrics, Kiki and Ray had a surprisingly domestic home life. While Ray posed his subjects in the studio, Kiki stayed upstairs, out of sight, waiting impatiently for him to be free. She was very impressed with Ray's guests, calling them "the aristocracy and the most famous people of the day." She could be wildly jealous, once rendering illegible all women's names in his address book. On occasion, if she suspected someone of flirting with Ray, she became physically violent.

Ray liked their strange domesticity, as he made evident in this passage from his memoirs:

> Kiki discovered a charming little flat in a courtyard back of the cafés, where some painter friends had their studios. . . . There was heat and a bathroom, which was rare in Paris. Kiki spent a good deal of time in the bathtub out of sheer luxury. Nearly always, when I dropped in during the day, I'd find her in a dressing gown or simply nude. If I announced that I had invited some friends for lunch or dinner, she went shopping and in no time had cooked a meal and set the table. The food was always delicious, good Burgundy dishes, plenty of wine, salads and carefully chosen cheeses. And as we sat around afterwards with glasses of brandy, she would sing us some popular Rabelaisian songs in a clear, perfectly

Kiki Cooks

tuned voice, accompanied by meaningful gestures and subtle facial expressions.

✶

The Found Meal for Kiki and Man Ray

BOEUF DAUBE À LA BOURGUIGNON
BOILED POTATOES
SALADE MESCLUN WITH GARLIC VINAIGRETTE
SELECTION OF FRENCH CHEESES
WINE

Boeuf Daube à la Bourguignon

The food of Burgundy is a lot like Kiki, who hailed from there: tasty, hearty, and generous. This beef stew, which uses Burgundy wine as one of its ingredients, has long been the region's most famous dish.

Sauté in butter over medium heat 2 pounds of good-quality boneless stewing beef cut into 1-inch cubes, and ½ pound thinly sliced salt pork. After a few minutes add ½ pound small boiling onions, peeled, and 1 minced garlic clove. Cook, stirring, until onions are lightly browned. Add 1 tablespoon tomato purée and stir. Sprinkle with 3 tablespoons flour and stir until it is absorbed by ingredients. Stir in 2 cups red Burgundy wine, 1½ cups beef stock or broth, 1 bay leaf, ½ teaspoon thyme, and 1 minced garlic clove. Cover and cook, very slowly, for 2½ hours. Stir occasionally. Salt and pepper to taste.

Boiled Potatoes

Boiled potatoes are traditionally served with Boeuf Bourguignon. See the recipe in the Gertrude Stein and Alice B. Toklas chapter, page 22.

Salade Mesclun

> Mesclun, a heady mixture of young lettuces, is one of the great culinary treats of France.

Choose a wide variety of very young greens, including, if possible, chicorée frisée and roquette (arugula). Other possibilities for inclusion are butter and romaine lettuces, dandelion greens, corn salad, and chervil. Toss with garlic vinaigrette, barely coating greens.

Garlic Vinaigrette

In a mortar, smash 3 large cloves of peeled garlic to a pulp. Then add ¼ cup olive oil, drop by drop, making a fine paste. Add 3 tablespoons red wine vinegar. Salt and pepper to taste.

A Few Words About French Cheese

It's common in France to be offered a selection of cheeses after the main dish and before (or in place of) dessert.

Kiki Cooks

More often than not you'll be presented with a handsome tray containing half a dozen or more cheeses.

To put together your own selection, choose a variety: soft, semi-soft, or runny; goat's, sheep's, or cow's milk; tart, mild, or bitter. Good choices might include Beaufort, Pont-l'Evèque, Brie, Saint-Marcellin, Camembert, Boursin, Rouquefort, Chèvre, or Munster.

Place the cheeses on a serving platter or tray an hour or so before serving, since they should be served at room temperature. Give each guest a small plate and knife. Keep the bread basket filled.

Suggested Wine

Burgundy—what else? Use up the rest of the cooking wine; or, if you're feeling daring, try a white Burgundy. One of the finest white Burgundies, Montrachet, is considered by many to be the world's greatest dry white wine.

Onion Soup, Les Halles, and the Dawn

*L*et's say you could climb into a time machine and be whisked off to Paris in the twenties. It's early evening, and you've landed unseen in a discreet corner of the Montparnasse cemetery. Your clothing has magically altered during the short journey from the century's other end, and you now affect the casual look popular at the time in artsy Parisian circles. If you're a man, you're clad in corduroy pants, dirty white sneakers, a casual and somewhat sloppy jacket. If you're a woman, you're in a straight, short dress with a dropped waist, have a long rope of pearls knotted below the neck, and are wearing t-strap shoes with small heels. You glance at your early-model wristwatch with its tiny numerals: it's 6:00 and you must return to the machine in twelve hours or you'll vanish forever in a puff of smoke.

So, what will you do with your time? How can you be sure to have the ultimate 1920s Parisian experience? Let's examine the possibilities.

You may want to start with a Pernod or two at the Select; perhaps while there you'll catch a glimpse of Hemingway or Djuna Barnes or Kay Boyle or Bob McAlmon, and maybe you'll even get into an argument with Madame Select herself (don't be alarmed; she argues with everybody). Then you may travel on to the latest trendy bar tended by Jimmie—is it the Jockey this month, or the Dingo? Josephine Baker and *La Revue Nègre* have recently arrived from Harlem to set *le tout Paris* abuzz with rhythm, so you won't want to miss that. And later you'll certainly want to drop into Cocteau's new place, Le Boeuf sur le Toit; here you can eat a fine meal as you watch the young French avant garde cavort about the dance floor. Then there's Bricktop's, with its great American jazz and maybe a glimpse of Cole Porter or the Prince of Wales. Bricktop's is busy until dawn, and the food is free along about three in the morning.

But, as good as it is, skip Bricktop's food and go somewhere else to eat. Because before you climb into that time machine for a quick trip home, you must have the quintessential 1920s expatriate experience: onion soup at dawn in Les Halles.

Les Halles—the gigantic wholesale produce, seafood, and meat market in the center of Paris—no longer exists, but it looms large in the memoirs of the time. Here at dawn came the owners of small food shops, the *chefs de cuisine* of fine hotels, and the thrifty *ménagères*, all in search of the best goods at the lowest prices. The markets were surrounded by inexpensive restaurants frequented by gangsters, prostitutes, and pimps, as well as the market's workers, slumming socialites, and many—oh, so many—American expatriates. Among these restaurants were Pied de Mouton, Pharamond, and Au Père Tranquille, all of which specialized in a thick and hearty onion soup.

Paris on Parade, a popular 1925 guidebook for visiting Americans, had this to say about the markets:

> The vicinity of Les Halles swarms with good restaurants, the chief speciality of which is onion soup, a thick savory mess which has the virtue of appealing to the appetite at its most jaded ebb. It has therefore become the fashion with the frivolous after a night spent with the gaieties and champagne of Montmartre to repair to Les Halles at dawn for la soupe à l'oignon.
>
> At that hour the market is at its height. The wide streets that run between the market buildings are jammed with porters, *commissionaires* (a fine word meaning errand men), market people and wholesale and retail buyers. . . . Truck drivers swear, crack their whips and shout "Attention!" for a right of way through the foot throng. Trucks cut out their mufflers and force passages by sheer frightfulness. Commissionaires drag carts or push hand trucks into the jam. Porters stagger under heaven-kissing loads piled on the carrying frames strapped to their backs. And through the sweatered, aproned, overalled throng go numerous glittering parties—bare shoulders and white shirtfronts—progressing arm in arm a trifle more animatedly than really sober folk

should do, for the onion soup that is to send them to bed physically comforted.

In 1926 Basil Woon, in his book *The Paris That's Not in the Guide Books*, described a long evening in which he and his friends had dinner at the elegant Pré Catalan, shared a bottle or two of champagne at Acacias, traveled on to Perroquet (decor by famed couturier Paul Poiret) for drinks, visited the Abbaye in Place Pigalle for even more drinks, braved the pimps and prostitutes along the rue Pigalle to get to Zelli's with its thirty dancing girls, and, finally:

... We pile into a taxi and head for the market and onion soup.

Onion soup is the traditional breakfast of the dichard, and the market the traditional place to eat it in. For onion soup is a soup that you eat.

The market is literally that. It is the great central produce exchange of Paris, and one picks one's way to the Père Tranquil's or to one of the other places over piles of cabbages and carrots and other vegetables, while hulking market porters glare at the décolleté and jewels of the women and mutter "sale bourgeois" under their breath.

They don't mean anything by that. They all hope to be dirty bourgeois themselves, one of these days.

As far as our American expatriates go, their memoirs and novels are thick with references to Les Halles. Margaret Anderson and others were frequently taken by the sculptor Brancusi for onion soup at dawn after a night of revels. Robert McAlmon wrote of being at Bricktop's with Man Ray, Kiki, and Nina Hamnett on the night Leon Crutcher, Bricktop's piano player, was shot to death by his French girlfriend. Afterward McAlmon and a few others went drinking, finally ending up in Les Halles, where, walking through the market's early-morning bustle, they met two prostitutes and spirited them away for *soupe à l'oignon*.

Harry Crosby made frequent reference to Les Halles in his diaries, as shown in this 1925 entry:

> ... champagne orangeades at the Ritz and after-wards to dance in the Bois and to dance in the Mont-martre and finally at dawn to Les Halles where we were the only two dancers. Seven o'clock and the end of the last bottle of champagne and a crazy bargain with a sturdy peasant to haul us to the Ritz in his vegetable cart and thus we reclined Geraldine in her silverness I in my blackness, upon the heaped-up carrots and cabbages while our poor man strained in the harness. A memorable ride with the strong sum-mer Sun streaming through the streets, she frivolous and gay, I pale as her dress, with champagne eyes and tousled hair.

In the end, Les Halles came to symbolize what it meant to be young in Paris in the twenties: dancing 'til dawn, onion soup at Pied de Mouton or Pharamond, and then home at last to bed, usually to start the same thing all over again the next night. When the twenties passed, so did the heydey of the markets as a social mecca.

In the 1930s the English journalist Sisley Huddleston ran into a friend from the old Montparnasse days. When the friend invited him to dinner, Huddleston teased him: in the old days we often dined at midnight, he said; should I come at midnight? "Midnight!" the friend scoffed, and then turned to dreamy recollections of his youth:

> Why, we had often not dined when the cafés closed at two o'clock in the morning, and we had to walk to the Halles and eat an onion soup in the open air before turning in. Ah, well, we dine regularly now at eight o'clock and usually go to bed between ten and eleven.

*

The Found Meal for Tout le Monde

ONION SOUP LES HALLES

———

Onion Soup Les Halles

One of the popular twenties restaurants of Les Halles was l'Escargot, which sometimes offered a soup made of red rather than yellow onions.

Melt 3 tablespoons olive oil and 1 tablespoon butter in large heavy saucepan over low heat. When butter and oil are hot, add 6 cups sliced red onions. Cook onions, covered, 20 minutes or until tender. Uncover, raise heat to medium, add 1 teaspoon salt, a few grinds of pepper, and 1 tablespoon sugar; continue cooking, stirring occasionally, until onions are golden brown. Sprinkle onions with 3 tablespoons flour and mix gently 2 to 3 minutes to cook the flour. Remove pan from heat temporarily, slowly adding 8 cups boiling beef stock and 1 cup dry white wine. Return to low heat and simmer, partially covered, 30 to 40 minutes. Just before serving, stir 3 tablespoons cognac into soup.

While soup cooks, brush olive oil and rub halved garlic clove onto four slices crusty French bread. Place bread on baking sheet in preheated 325° oven for 15 minutes, just until bread is dry and lightly browned.

When ready to serve, pour very hot soup into individual oven-proof soup tureens; float slice of French bread on top, spreading over it 2 tablespoons of grated Gruyère cheese. Sprinkle with a little olive oil and slip beneath broiler until cheese has browned lightly. Serve at once.

NATALIE CLIFFORD BARNEY:
At the Salon of Natalie Barney

E ven by today's standards Natalie Barney stands out as a brilliantly unconventional figure. For almost one hundred years she shattered tradition and defied societal icons. Her uninhibited and emancipated life made her the thinly disguised heroine of at least six novels, the subject of two biographies, and a major entrant in scores of memoirs from the *belle époque* to the present day. To say she lived fully seems somehow inadequate, as she herself admitted: "Having got more out of life, oh having got out of it perhaps more than it contained!"

Barney was born in 1876 to a wealthy Ohio family descended from railroad tycoons, naval heroes, judges, and bank presidents. Her father was highly conventional, but her mother, an accomplished painter who had studied in Paris with Whistler, bordered on the bohemian. The family moved to Washington, D.C., when Natalie was ten, thereafter summering in Bar Harbor and taking frequent jaunts to Europe. Natalie fell in love with Paris and, by her late teens, visited the city often.

By this time Natalie was a beautiful young woman with long, billowing masses of blonde hair, a willowy figure, and amused blue eyes. She loved fashion, favoring white gowns by Poiret. She spoke fluent, beautifully accented French, as well as German and Italian. She was a proficient violinist, a superb horsewoman (accounting for her life-long nickname, the Amazon), and a budding poet with a reputation for witty repartee. Needless to say, she was heavily courted by eligible young men.

Natalie, however, preferred to do the courting, and, as her interest in men was only "from the neck up," it was women who received her favors. Attracted to women since childhood, Natalie was quite open about her lesbianism. She had lovers through her teens, but it wasn't until the late 1890s that she had her first serious love affair. While horseback riding one day in the Bois de Boulogne she caught sight of Liane de Pougy, the most famous of all *belle époque* courtesans. Struck by the older woman's beauty and elegance, the teenage Natalie determined to seduce her. Against all odds, she did just that. The two beauties made no secret of their passionate affair, which blazed in the face of *tout* Paris.*

When Natalie's father learned of the affair, he summoned her immediately back to Washington, D.C., and insisted that she marry. But before a suitable husband could be found, her father died. Natalie, having inherited 2.5 million dollars, returned to Paris a very wealthy young woman.

---

*Liane de Pougy would later write about their affair in her novel, *Idylle Sapphique*, a French *success de scandale* in the early years of this century.

At the Salon of Natalie Barney

There were so many love affairs over the course of Natalie's long life—her last affair began when she was eighty-five—that she has been called a female Don Juan. Among her lovers were the poet Renée Vivien, with whom she traveled to Lesbos to honor Sappho, the painter Romaine Brooks, and the writers Dolly Wilde and Djuna Barnes. Natalie's passions usually ebbed quickly—usually much too quickly for her current love—and soon she would be pursuing her next conquest. She broke many hearts, in the process provoking threats, suicide attempts, and violent scenes. But Natalie had a rare gift for friendship, usually making lifelong friends of former lovers.

In 1909, when she was thirty-three, Natalie moved to 20, rue Jacob, a narrow seventeenth-century street on the edge of the Latin Quarter near St. Germain des Prés. The elegant little house, with its beautiful ironwork balconies, is said to have belonged originally to a mistress of Louis XIV. Natalie furnished rue Jacob with her mother's elaborate hand-me-downs: tapestries, velvet-covered love seats, gold-framed mirrors, a grand piano. The house was removed from the street by a deep courtyard, making it a quiet and discreet place for romantic assignations. The best thing about it was the overgrown garden with its small, Doric-columned temple whose entrance was crowned by the words "á l'amitié" carved into stone. American visitors called it the Temple of Friendship.*

---

*Today the Temple of Friendship is a national monument and cannot be altered without the express permission of the French government.

Twenty rue Jacob became a Paris landmark from the moment Natalie instituted her "Fridays," a literary salon attended by some of the foremost writers and thinkers of the century. Begun in 1909, the Salon continued almost uninterrupted for the next sixty years, undaunted even by the shelling of Paris during the Great War, the German invasion of 1941, or the nearby student riots of 1968.

By the twenties Natalie's Fridays provided an exciting and entertaining way for American and French writers to meet. The list of her American guests at this time reads like a *Who's Who* of twenties Paris: Ernest Hemingway, Scott and Zelda Fitzgerald, Sinclair Lewis, Sherwood Anderson, Janet Flanner, Edna St. Vincent Millay, Djuna Barnes, Isadora Duncan, Ford Madox Ford, William Carlos Williams, Sylvia Beach, Gertrude Stein, Alice B. Toklas, Ezra Pound, Virgil Thomson, Hart Crane, and George Antheil. The French came too, among them Colette, Adrienne Monnier, André Gide, Jean Cocteau, Max Jacob, Marie Laurencin, and Apollinaire. The composer George Antheil summed up Natalie in this period by saying her salon included "the elite of 1926, the rich and titled intellectuals who, more often than not, made modern art of all varieties in that city financially possible."

Perhaps because Natalie was a writer* the salon had a strong literary flavor. It didn't, however, confine itself to

---

*Natalie wrote ten books over a sixty-three-year period. Of particular merit are her three volumes of memoirs. The first, *Aventures de l'Esprit* (1929), discusses writers she had known to that date, including Oscar Wilde, Anatole France,

At the Salon of Natalie Barney

readings. Among the more memorable events were a troupe of nude Javanese dancers, George Antheil's première of his "First String Quartet," Colette and Paul Poiret acting the principal roles in Colette's *La Vagabonde* while accompanied by the famed harpsichordist Wanda Landowska, Virgil Thomson playing the piano and singing his own compositions, Gertrude Stein reading from *The Making of Americans* in English followed by Natalie reading her own translation in French, and Mata Hari riding naked through the gardens on a white horse harnessed with emeralds.

Many beautiful women attended the Fridays, most of them preferring each other's company. This sometimes didn't sit well with male guests like William Carlos Williams, who wrote:

> She [Natalie] was extremely gracious and no fool to be sure. . . . She could tell a pickle from a clam any day in the week. I admired her and her lovely garden, well kept, her laughing doves, her Japanese servants. There were officers wearing red buttons in their lapels there and women of all descriptions. Out of the corner of my eye I saw a small clique of them sneaking off together into a side room while casting surreptitious glances around them, hoping their exit had not been unnoticed. I went out and stood up to take a good piss.

Proust, and Rilke. *Souvenirs Indescrets* (1960) freely discusses her lovers, most of whom were dead by that time. *Traits et Portraits* (1963) is, like *Aventures*, a dissertation of writers, including André Gide, Jean Cocteau, and Gertrude Stein.

Refreshments were served on the dining-room table by Natalie's butler, a Frenchman who each day painted a head of curly black hair onto his bald pate. Most of the delicacies were prepared by Natalie's life-long housekeeper, Berthe. Interviewed by George Wickes, author of Barney's biography, *The Amazon of Letters*, Natalie's neighbor Eyre de Lanux recalled "the dining room, one wall of which led on to the garden, the green half-light of which came into the room, reflecting from the glasses and silver tea urn as from under water. A very large oval table—I suppose the cloth was lace—at one end the tea, the cups, and at the other, glass pitchers of fruit cup. I remember the triangular sandwiches and the harlequin-colored little cakes."

Another friend, Bettina Bergery, told Wickes of the "little cucumber sandwiches like damp handkerchiefs in memory of those served by Oscar Wilde and other poetic and delicious delicacies with semi-classic references." Those cucumber sandwiches must have been something really special: interviewed years later about Natalie Barney, Janet Flanner mentioned them four times in the space of an hour.

When Truman Capote made it to the salon in the late forties not much had changed: In an epilogue to Wickes's book, he recalled that "At Miss Barney's everyone met in a room with a huge domed ceiling of stained glass. The decor was totally turn-of-the-century, with a slightly Turkish quality about it—a kind of cross between a chapel and a bordello. There was always a big buffet on the side with the most marvelous things—I mean the most delicious kinds of strawberry and raspberry tarts in the dead of winter; and always champagne. Tea and champagne."

*

The Found Meal for the Salon of Natalie Barney

FRUIT CUPS
CUCUMBER SANDWICHES À LA OSCAR WILDE
STRAWBERRY AND RASPBERRY TARTS
CHAMPAGNE
TEA

Fruit Cups

Pick a selection of the best fruits in season—from berries, plums, melons, nectarines, and peaches in summer to bananas, oranges, pears, and apples in winter. Wash and dry; combine in a bowl, cutting larger fruits into bite-sized pieces. Add a liqueur such as black currant (Alice Toklas's recipe is on page 131), kirsch, or cassis—about 1 tablespoon for each serving. If desired, add a bit of very fine sugar. Mix fruit gently but thoroughly. Cover and chill for up to four hours. Mix fruit once more, spoon into small glass serving cups or bowls, and serve immediately.

Cucumber Sandwiches à la Oscar Wilde

It's best to make these sandwiches just before serving, since they tend to get soggy if they sit around.

To make 10 sandwiches, peel and very thinly slice 1 large English cucumber. Lay slices in a colander and sprinkle lightly with salt. Allow to sit 1 hour. Wipe slices completely dry with cloth or paper towel. Combine cucumber slices in a bowl with 1 tablespoon olive oil, 1 tablespoon lemon juice, ½ teaspoon sugar, and a bit of white pepper. Mix gently and let sit while you prepare the bread.

Take the highest-quality white or country bread available—preferably homemade and 1-day old—and slice it thinly; you'll need 20 slices. Slice off the crusts. In a bowl combine 1½ cups unsalted butter brought to room temperature, 2 tablespoons cream, and ½ teaspoon Dijon-style mustard. Mix thoroughly. Spread this filling generously on each piece of bread; arrange cucumber slices on half the bread slices, top with the remaining 10 slices. Cut the sandwich in half on the diagonal, forming 2 triangles. Arrange the triangles on a serving plate surrounded with sprigs of watercress.

Strawberry and Raspberry Tarts

Small, individual fruit tarts, or tartlets, are found in every French *boulangerie*. This recipe makes 12 small tarts.

To make tart pastry, cut up 2 sticks (½ pound) butter and let soften. In a mixing bowl, combine 2 cups flour with 1½ tablespoons sugar; cut butter into the flour with a fork until it resembles very coarse meal. In a separate bowl, combine ⅛ teaspoon almond extract and ⅛ teaspoon vanilla extract with 2 tablespoons water; stir into flour. Gather dough into a ball, flatten slightly, wrap in waxed paper and chill in refrigerator for 1 hour; then let dough stand at room temperature until malleable. Press into 12 buttered tart shells or shallow muffin pans, forming ⅛-inch crusts. Press fork tines against rims, giving texture.

Prepare 2 cups each strawberries and raspberries. Wash and dry berries, putting them in separate bowls and sprinkling each bowl with 1 tablespoon of sugar (if the berries are very juicy, combine sugar with 1 teaspoon arrowroot before sprinkling). Fill half the tart shells with raspberries and the rest with strawberries. Bake in preheated 375° oven for 35–45 minutes, until crusts are golden. Tarts will unmold easily, as pastry will have shrunk away from sides of pan during baking.

Champagne

You'll find a brief discussion on French champagne on page 200.

Tea

A discussion on the preparation of tea is contained on page 56.

JOHN DOS PASSOS AND
ERNEST HEMINGWAY:

At the Cycle Races

What marathon dances were to the United States in the twenties, six-day cycle races were to France ... sort of. The similarities were that the players, while watched by a crowd of onlookers, tried to keep moving as long as possible, sleeping only when absolutely necessary. Whether dancing or biking, those who stayed up the longest won a large sum of money.

The differences were many. The bicyclists were always professional athletes, whereas the dancers were usually young kids in need of money. The dances tended to receive mostly tabloid newspaper coverage, whereas the bike races dominated French newspapers, radio, and many magazines. Perhaps the greatest difference of all lay in the onlookers: in the United States marathon dance attendees were mostly poor. In France, those who watched the cyclists defied social and economic categorization.

In Paris the races were held at the Vélodrome d'Hiver, a large gymnasium located near the Eiffel Tower. Few spectators watched for all six days, of course; some came only once, while others dropped in frequently. For a few francs you could buy yourself a spot in the bleachers, bring a picnic, and hang out as long as you liked. For a lot more francs, you could sit in the raised gallery and—while drinking champagne or enjoying dinner—gaze down at the cyclists' eternal circling around the wooden track. Journalist Sisley Huddleston once described the event:

> An extraordinary Parisian Nights Entertainment is provided by the Six Days Cycle Race at the Vélodrome d'Hiver. . . . There while the unfortunate cyclists turn like squirrels, a motley throng assembles. It is after midnight that the spectacle is most astonishing. There is the populace of Paris, witty but impertinent, shouting encouragement and insult. There are the elegant revellers of Paris, befurred and bediamonded. The rich onlookers offer prizes to the competitors, and when they are not generous enough the "populaires" hurl violent apostrophes at them, treating the women as "poules de luxe." The contrast between the rich idlers in their loggias, with their champagne before them, and the masses in the galleries is amazing. A crude white light falls on this strange scene. The "squirrels" turn, turn . . .

One who loved to attend the cycle races—as well as boxing bouts, tennis matches, and bullfights—was Ernest Hemingway, himself an excellent athlete. The journalist William Shirer was surprised when first meeting Hemingway because he did not look or talk much like a writer. He was big and athletic, with a ruddy complexion and bright, lively eyes. Turning to me he began to talk of sports: the six-day bicycle races at the Velodrome d'Hiver, the fights at the Cirque de Paris and a new French middleweight boxer he thought might make it, the tennis and Suzanne Lenglen, the graceful, vivacious French champion. He was playing a lot of tennis, he said, and doing even more boxing. . . . He said not a word about writing, which I was hoping he would, for like most of the young Americans in Paris I was already trying to write.

Whenever possible, Hemingway brought his friends to athletic events. Sometimes the combination of event and person was a bit incongruous, as when he took the gentle Sylvia Beach and her companion Adrienne Monnier to a boxing match ("We were afraid they were going to bleed to death," she wrote), but usually everybody had a good time. Hemingway, apparently, could be wonderful company.

For a while in the early twenties Hemingway and John Dos Passos frequently spent time together, hiking cross-country or attending athletic events. Dos Passos recalled their visit to the Vélo:

> I did enjoy going to the six day bicycle races with him [Hemingway]. The Six Jours at the Vélo d'Hiver was fun. French sporting events had for me a special comical air that I enjoyed. We would collect, at the

stalls and barrows of one of the narrow market streets we both loved, a quantity of wine and cheeses and crunch rolls, a pot of paté and perhaps a cold chicken, and sit up in the gallery. Hem knew all the statistics and the names and lives of the riders. His enthusiasm was catching but he tended to make a business of it while I just liked to eat and drink and to enjoy the show.

✶

The Found Meal for John Dos Passos and Ernest Hemingway

RABBIT PÂTÉ
COLD ROAST CHICKEN
SELECTION OF FRENCH CHEESES
FRENCH BAGUETTE OR CRUSTY ROLLS
WINE

Rabbit Pâté

The recipe for rabbit pâté is derived from a twenties version served at Hotel of the Hunt in Villers-Cotterets, a small village near Paris. The original recipe appeared in the 1926 *Epicurean Yellow Guide to Paris and Environs.*

Bone a nice-sized rabbit. Cut breast and loin into long, thin slices and marinate overnight in mixture of ¼ cup dry white wine, 2 tablespoons brandy or cognac, 2 table-spoons olive oil, and ½ sliced onion, a pinch of thyme, and 1 chopped garlic clove. Chop rest of rabbit meat, including liver, into very fine dice. Combine with 1 pound fatty ground pork, ½ cup dry white wine, 1 tablespoon brandy, 2 tablespoons olive oil, a pinch of nutmeg, 1 teaspoon salt, and ½ teaspoon ground pepper. Blend well, cover, and let rest in refrigerator overnight.

Line a covered pâté mold or terrine with strips of pork fat ⅛-inch thick. Remove breast and loin pieces from marinade and put temporarily aside. Add forcemeat mixture to marinade, blend thoroughly, and divide into thirds. Spread ⅓ mixture in bottom of terrine. Decoratively arrange ⅓ slices breast and loin atop forcemeat. Continue alternating layers, ending with third layer of breast and loin. Cover with last layer of pork fat; lay a few sprigs of thyme atop fat. Cover with tin foil and then with terrine's lid; place in larger pan; fill larger pan with boiling water until it comes halfway up outside of terrine. Set in lower third of oven preheated to 350° and bake approximately 1½ hours. Pâté is done when it has shrunk away from terrine sides and the surrounding juices contain no hint of red coloring. Place a weight on terrine and let cool several hours. Serve directly from terrine or unmolded on plate.

At the Cycle Races

Cold Roast Chicken

Follow the recipe for roast chicken on page 183. Enjoy half of it fresh from the oven; refrigerate the second half, using it the next day for your Found Meal.

A Selection of French Cheeses

French cheese is discussed in the Kiki/Man Ray chapter, page 80.

Suggested Wine

A crisp and dry white—an Entre-deux-mers or a Muscadet, for example—would go well with this picnic.

JIMMIE THE BARMAN:
Aphrodisia

He was an ex-flyweight boxer from Liverpool who thought Americans were the friendliest people in the world. "I liked them very much," he said about the dozens of G.I.s he'd met during the war, "[they were] always ready for a drink and a good time, or for a fight."

A drink, a good time, and a fight: that was James Charters in a nutshell. Server of the best drinks in the best-time, brawlingest bars of Montparnasse, he was known to an entire generation of Americans as simply Jimmie the Barman. Generous and pugnacious, Jimmie was so popular that his presence behind the counter could sextuple a bar's daily intake. He changed jobs frequently, eventually putting his stamp on the Dingo, the Jockey, Hole in the Wall, and Trois et As, among a dozen others. His friends and customers were the likes of Sylvia Beach, Ernest Hemingway, Bob McAlmon, Laurence Vail, Peggy Guggenheim, Kay Boyle, Djuna Barnes, James Joyce, Man Ray, Kiki, Nina Hamnett, Lady Duff Twysden, Isadora Duncan, Jean Cocteau, Marcel Duchamp, Hart Crane, and Sinclair Lewis.

Perhaps Jimmie was so popular because of his enthusiasm for the Montparnasse scene, as illustrated by this passage from his memoirs:

I had never been in a madhouse before I went to Montparnasse. I had never seen people drink to get drunk; never seen artists, writers, nobles, American sailors, and doubtful women mingle on equal terms without reserve . . . all talking together, all friends without class consciousness, all learning from each other, all professing an interest in art with a big A. . . . During an evening with such a crowd I would listen to details of a recent prize fight, details of how a young man should treat a girl in bed, details of a scheme for a trans-atlantic air-mail route, details of a suicide—there were always plenty of details!

He was also popular because he was good at what he did. Ernest Hemingway—a legendary drinker—considered Jimmie such an excellent barman that he said so in an introduction to Charters's memoirs. Samuel Putnam recalled in *Paris Was Our Mistress* that Jimmie would put up with impossibly drunk and obnoxious customers far longer than necessary. But even this patient man could be pushed beyond his limits. When the ex-flyweight had taken enough, Putnam wrote, he'd simply plant a professional punch and put the unruly celebrant to sleep

as gently and as painlessly as possible; after which, he would go out in front of the bar, pick the chap up, dust him off, and—as soon as the victim had regained consciousness—apologize to him. He then would call a taxi, with directions to the chauffeur to see the man safely home, and to top it all, would pay the fare! Is it any wonder that we loved him?

In his memoirs Jimmie offers many insights into the bartending trade. Of particular fascination is his breakdown of artistic drinking types: painters and photographers, he says, are the heaviest, noisiest drinkers, followed by journalists; the most depressed are sculptors; and most imbibers of white wine are writers. He professes much admiration for those who drink straight whiskey and, in a gesture of typical generosity, gives away the secret for his most famous drink:

> And now comes the question that I have been asked many times, often for a purpose: What drinks are aphrodisiac? . . . I must tell you of a cocktail I invented while I was at the Dingo that had a powerful effect on some of the Quarterites . . . two stiff drinks of it will have some surprising effects! . . .
>
> On women this drink had the effect of causing them to undress in public, and it often kept me busy wrapping overcoats around nude ladies! But even knowing this did not prevent some of the feminine contingent from asking for the Jimmie Special. I wish I had a hundred francs for every nude or semi-nude lady I've wrapped up during the best Montparnasse days!

The Found Meal for Jimmie the Bartender

THE JIMMIE SPECIAL

———

The Jimmie Special

For two people, combine in a cocktail shaker: 1 jigger cognac, ½ jigger Pernod, ½ jigger Amer-Picon, ½ jigger Mandarin, and ½ jigger sweet cherry brandy (kirsch). Shake thoroughly. Drink straight or mix with soda to taste.

DJUNA BARNES:

Salad Days

L awrence Durrell claimed he was glad to be alive in the same epoch that produced Djuna Barnes. Former U.N. Secretary-General Dag Hammarskjöld believed she deserved the Nobel Prize for Literature. Dylan Thomas said that Barnes's *Nightwood* was one of the three greatest prose books ever written by a woman. James Joyce honored her with the original, highly annotated manuscript of *Ulysses*. And the journalist Janet Flanner said that she was the most important woman writer of her time living in Paris, famous among Left Bank writers.*

Given this praise, it's amazing that Barnes's work isn't better known today. Perhaps it's because, as Sylvia Beach once remarked, she wasn't one to "cry her wares." She does have a following, however, and there are signs that it's still growing today. *Nightwood*, her most famous work, has never gone out of print since its publication in 1936. Other books have been re-issued periodically: *Ladies Al-*

---

*References to Djuna Barnes as a "woman writer" rather than as simply a writer are irritating by today's standards, but were common in the twenties.

manack and *Spillway* in 1972, a collection of journalistic pieces in 1985, and the novel *Ryder* in 1990.

Born in 1892 in upper New York State, Barnes came to New York in 1911 to study art at the Pratt Institute. That year her first poems were published in *Harper's Weekly*, which encouraged her to pursue writing. She soon obtained minor fame writing for top magazines like *Smart Set* and *Vanity Fair*, where her interviews with celebrities such as Lillian Russell and Diamond Jim Brady appeared. By mid-decade she had moved to Greenwich Village, where she wrote plays and short stories. The Providence Playhouse performed three Barnes plays in 1919 and 1920; others were published in leading literary magazines, as were her poems, illustrations, and stories.

In 1921 Barnes moved to Paris, staying first at the Hôtel d'Angleterre along with Man Ray, Berenice Abbott, Sherwood Anderson, Marcel Duchamp, and Harold Loeb, most of whom she knew from the Village. The tall, good-looking Barnes fell quickly into the Montparnasse scene. She was popular but not uniformly well liked; admirers spoke of her wit and charm, while detractors considered her snobbish, rude, and emotionally shallow. Margaret Anderson once said of Barnes that she was "not on speaking terms with her own psyche."

In time Barnes found an apartment on the Boulevard St.-Germain where she lived with her new lover, Thelma Wood, a silverpoint artist with an alcoholic bent and a rakehell character. Wood, whose physical beauty is frequently remarked upon in memoirs of the time, often left people staring in her wake when she raced her red Bugatti through the narrow Parisian streets.

The decade-long relationship between the two women was characterized on the one hand by love, devotion, and tenderness; on the other by excessive drinking and violence. Wood's capacity for liquor was extraordinary. She would drink all day and all night, finally picking up a handsome/pretty stranger and disappearing with him/her, perhaps for a day, perhaps a week. On the nights Thelma didn't come home—and there were many—Djuna conducted desperate searches of bars, cafés, and bistros. The recriminations, jealousy, and anger were brutal, finally destroying their love. *Nightwood*, published in 1936, was based largely on Barnes's relationship with Wood.

But, despite personal trauma and Barnes's own problems with alcohol, the twenties were a productive time for her. *A Book*, a collection of short stories, poems, and theater pieces, was published in 1923 to critical praise. *Ryder*, a dark, bleak novel lavish and ornate in style, appeared in 1928 and set the literary world on its ear: *The Saturday Review* called it "The most amazing book ever written by a woman"; *transition* said it was "a work of grim, mature beauty [that] no women, and few men, have succeeded in giving us"; *The Argonaut* described it as "vulgar, beautiful, defiant, witty, poetic, and a little mad . . . the most amazing thing to have come from a woman's hand."

Ryder, which Barnes illustrated, was censored by U.S. customs officials for obscenity; it couldn't be distributed in the States unless specific drawings and words were deleted. Barnes insisted the offending words be replaced with asterisks so the reading public would be shown "where the war, so blindly waged on the written word, has left its mark." Despite its strictures (or perhaps because of them), *Ryder* attained best-sellerdom in the United States.

Ladies Almanack, a small chapbook crammed with woodcuts and disguised characterizations, was privately printed in 1928, the author's name acknowledged only as "A Lady of Fashion." *Ladies Almanack* is a clever and lusty satire about a group of lesbians. The style is ornately Elizabethan and, like much of Barnes's work, takes place in nonchronological fashion. The central character, Evangeline Musset, who is admired by and presides over the other women, is based on her close friend Natalie Barney. All the other characters have real-life counterparts, as well; among those caricatured are Janet Flanner, Lady Una Trowbridge, Mina Loy, Dolly Wilde (Oscar's niece), Esther Murphy (sister of Gerald), Solita Solano, and Radclyffe Hall. In this passage from *Ladies Almanack*, Barnes's Elizabethan style is in evidence:

Winter feast on Summer starve bring all Brooks to churning, and pass the Whey as ever you may, your Hands will print the Butterspot on the Foolscap of confession. So eat your Winter Lettuce, and say your Spring Beads, seek your Mirror, or stand in the cold at the hour of Midnight, or put what you will under your Pillow to know what you can in the Dawn of it, or see the Moon over your Shoulder, roving and hunting the world for an Omen, you'll get her, you'll have her, you'll take her and lose her, you'll miss by an Item, and over-reach by a Yard, undervalue, over-estimate, hot bed or cold! The Branch does not bend unless for a passing, and some must go first, and some must come after. And how is the Jungle so twig-thick and underfoot, if not because a Bison, and a Bison and a Bison went by?

✳

The Found Meal for Djuna Barnes

A SALAD OF WINTER LETTUCES

A Salad of Winter Lettuces

Bravig Imbs provided the inspiration for this salad. In his memoirs, *Confessions of Another Young Man*, he recalled eating a salad composed of celery, endive, lettuce, cinquefoil, and watercress. Cinquefoil, a member of the rose family, grows wild in the United States.

In a small bowl combine 1 tablespoon walnut oil, 2 tablespoons high-quality olive oil, 1 tablespoon raspberry vinegar, and 1 finely minced shallot. Let flavors blend while preparing the salad.

Cut away and discard the stem of two large Belgian endives, removing whole leaves. Discard stems of 1 bunch watercress, breaking into sprigs. Tear 1 frisée endive into pieces (or equivalent amount of curly endive). Wash and dry all greens and place in salad bowl. Peel a small celeriac, slice it thinly, and cut slices into strips; add no more than ½ cup celeriac strips to greens. Pour dressing over salad and toss gently. Just before serving, sprinkle petals of 1 perfect red rose across the salad.

1924

In Paris

Steamship companies reduce European fare by creating "tourist third class"; artists and students by the thousands come to Paris . . . Arrivals: Langston Hughes, Bricktop, Scott and Zelda Fitzgerald (second visit), William Carlos Williams . . . George Antheil composes *Ballet Mécanique* . . . Jimmie becomes barman at the Dingo; a few months later F. Scott Fitzgerald and Ernest Hemingway meet there for the first time . . . Fitzgerald estimates he has made and spent $113,000 in the last four years and is now $5,000 in debt . . . Caresse and Harry Crosby establish Black Sun Press . . . Paris publication of Hemingway's *in our time* and *Antheil and the Treatise on Harmony* by Ezra Pound (both by Three Mountains Press) . . . First issue of Ford Madox Ford's *Transatlantic Review* . . . Ernest Hemingway, Donald Ogden Stewart, and John Dos Passos participate in the running of the bulls in Pamplona, Spain . . .

LANGSTON HUGHES:

In the Garret

Attracted by the relaxed French attitude toward race, many black Americans came to Paris in the twenties, forming a significant community of their own. In France blacks could sit anywhere they wanted on a bus or in a theater, and were welcome in every restaurant in town. In France, also, black and white could mingle romantically without fear of life. Among the inter-racial couples of the time were the aristocratic English-woman Nancy Cunard and the black pianist Henry Crowder, and Josephine Baker and the French mystery writer Georges Simenon (and, later, a spurious European count who became her first husband).

But even in France things weren't perfect. Blacks competed not only with the French but with white Americans for the best jobs, usually losing out in the process. If you were black and could sing the blues, play hot jazz, or tap dance, you were virtually assured of work; if not, dish-washing and waiting on tables was bound to be your lot. There was also the not-infrequent danger of running into a visiting American bigot who refused—sometimes with physical violence, *always* embarrassingly—to sit beside you in a restaurant. And, though many white American bohemians professed tolerance or at least lack of overt bigotry, they basically held themselves aloof from their darker skinned compatriots: it is the rare white memoir of the time that mentions a black person in any capacity other than entertainer.

When he arrived in Paris in 1924, the nascent poet Langston Hughes had seven dollars in his pocket. He was twenty-two years old and had left behind not only his studies at Columbia University, but also his deep involvement with the black artistic movement known as the Harlem Renaissance. He had come to Paris for the same reason many of his white compatriots had: he wanted to live cheaply and write in the capital of modernism. In time Hughes would be called the most influential black American writer of the century; he would explore virtually every form of literature by writing poetry, novels, short stories, plays, autobiography, television scripts, and journalism; and he would win both a Guggenheim Fellowship and the Harmon Award for Literature.

At the moment, though, wandering through the icy February streets of Paris, Hughes was cold, hungry, and broke. In his autobiography, *The Big Sea*, he recalled searching for a job that first day. Unable to speak French, he had little luck. Finally, seeing a group of black musicians outside a club, he asked for advice in finding a job.

"You must be crazy, boy," one of the men said. "There ain't no 'any kind of a job' here. There're plenty of

French people for ordinary work. 'Less you can play jazz or tap dance, you'd just as well go back home."

Hughes eventually landed work as dishwasher in a run-down nightclub called Le Grand Duc. The Duc wasn't one of the more popular clubs in town, but sometimes Fred and Adele Astaire or Nancy Cunard dropped in; Hughes gazed wistfully at these luminaries from the kitchen, little imagining that, ten years later, Cunard would include a number of his poems in her important 1934 *Negro Anthology*. It was while working at Le Grand Duc—listening nightly to such great musicians as the pianist Palmer Jones, trumpeter Cricket Smith, and drummer Buddy Gilmore—that Hughes decided to incorporate jazz rhythms into his poems. Today his works are famous for their short, direct lyrics infused with the cadence of blues, jazz, and gospel.

So much did Hughes enjoy his Paris stay that, in *The Big Sea*, he equated it with a fantasy straight out of fiction. Not only was he living in an artist's garret, writing poetry, and drinking champagne for breakfast, but he fell in love in Paris in the spring. His lover was Mary, a beautiful woman of African and English descent. Her father, strongly objecting to her involvement with a dishwasher, ordered her back to London. In his autobiography Hughes recalled their last night together, dining in a little restaurant near Sacre-Coeur:

We had wine and épaule de veau and a salade de saison and coeur à la crème. And then we went walking

In the Garret

down the winding old streets of the hill, and across the Boulevard Clichy. And somehow we came to my house, and we went climbing up the steep stairs in the cool, half-dark hall, up, up, up, until we came to where the roof slanted and my room was under the eaves.

On the way to the house we had seen a pile of tiny strawberries, the wild French fraises de bois, in a grocer's window, so we bought a paper coneful, and two little jars of yellow cream. And we sat in my room on the wide stone window seat, in an open gabled window that looked over the chimney pots of Paris, and ate the strawberries and cream, dipping each berry into the cream and feeding each other, and sadly watching the sun set over Paris. And we felt very *tristes* and very young and helpless, because we could not do what we wanted to do—be happy together.

*

The Found Meal for Langston Hughes

ÉPAULE DE VEAU FARCI
SALADE FRISÉE WITH LARDOONS AND POACHED EGG
COEUR À LA CRÈME
FRAISES DE BOIS DIPPED IN CRÈME FRAÎCHE
WINE

Épaule de Veau Farci

Bone a medium-sized veal shoulder, trimming fat; place waxed paper over meat and pound with rolling pin to form a rectangular-shaped piece of uniform thickness. Season to taste with salt and pepper. In a bowl combine ¼ pound ground veal, ¼ pound ground pork or chopped ham (including some ham fat), 1 beaten egg, ¼ cup fresh breadcrumbs and 2 tablespoons brandy. Spread mixture over veal, roll up, and tie with string in three or four places. Heat 2 tablespoons vegetable oil in heavy pan; brown meat on all sides. Pour off excess fat. Add boiling beef or veal stock to depth of 1½ inches and allow liquid to come to boil again; immediately reduce heat, cover and let simmer. It may be necessary to add stock again; it should always stay at the same level. Turn meat from time to time.

Allow to cook 1½ hours. At this point you may add chopped carrots, potatoes, and/or onions. Return to simmer for another ½ hour. Remove meat to serving dish; surround with vegetables and keep warm. Meanwhile, rapidly boil cooking liquid until it thickens. Pour over meat and vegetables and serve.

Salade Frisée with Lardoons and Poached Egg

Prepare dressing by combining 2 tablespoons red wine vinegar, 1 clove finely chopped garlic, and 1 teaspoon Dijon mustard in small bowl. Slowly beat in 5 tablespoons high-quality olive oil, drop by drop. Season with salt and freshly ground pepper to taste.

Toast 4 slices bread under broiler; when browned and slightly dried, rub lightly with halved garlic clove and cut into cubes. Set aside.

In large skillet, cook ½ pound slab bacon cut into bite-sized squares. Stir frequently and cook until crisp. Remove from pan onto paper towels. Set aside.

Divide onto 4 salad plates frisée or curly endive that has been washed, dried, and torn into small pieces. Divide croutons and bacon between plates, spooning dressing over all. Sprinkle generously with freshly ground pepper.

Poach 4 eggs (follow instructions on page 163). When done, remove each egg with a slotted spoon, placing gently atop salads. Serve immediately.

Coeur à la Crème

To make the coeur (or cream heart), it's necessary to have a heart-shaped mold with draining holes in the bottom. A well-stocked cooking store can provide you with a porcelain mold such as this, and some antique stores may have heart-shaped baskets (cover the bottom wickerwork with a layer of cheesecloth before filling with the coeur). If all else fails, let the coeur drain overnight in a collander, packing it next day into a heart-shaped mold of your own making fashioned from cardboard heavily covered with tinfoil.

Combine in a bowl 1 pound natural cream cheese, 2 tablespoons heavy cream, and a generous pinch of salt. Beat together vigorously until mixture has feeling of lightness. Add 1 cup sour cream and mix thoroughly. Pour mixture into heart-shaped mold, cover mold with waxed paper, and set in a bowl to catch the petit-lait that will drain off. Place in refrigerator overnight. When ready to serve, unmold cheese onto clear glass serving dish and surround with fresh strawberries, raspberries, or blackberries.

Fraises de Bois Dipped in Crème Fraîche

If you can't find fraises de bois—tiny wild strawberries—choose instead the smallest, ripest strawberries available. Rinse in cold water and place in glass or ceramic serving bowl with smaller bowl of crème fraîche on the side. If you desire, sprinkle strawberries with a light dusting of very fine sugar.

Prepare crème fraîche a day ahead by pouring 1 pint heavy cream into a glass jar; add 1 tablespoon buttermilk and stir well. Cover and let the jar stand overnight in a warm place. Before serving, you may want to gently whisk in a few drops of vanilla to the crème.

GERTRUDE STEIN:

At the Salon of Gertrude Stein

T he war years changed Gertrude Stein's Paris. Picasso had grown rich and famous; now married to a former dancer with the Russian ballet, he lived in an expensive Right Bank apartment and wore hand-tailored suits. Apollinaire was dead, a victim of influenza; Matisse had moved to the south of France; Juan Gris was ill; and Braque was on the outs with just about everybody. The days of easy, youthful friendship were gone.

But the decade brought new friends—literary rather than artistic, American rather than European. First among them was Sylvia Beach, whom Gertrude met in 1920 shortly after Shakespeare and Company opened for business. They quickly became friends.

Though the majority of Stein's work remained unpublished, she was now, by virtue of being constantly talked about, the most famous American writer living in Paris. Many writers resented her fame; Robert McAlmon, for instance, considered her to be merely a phony with a genius for presenting herself as an exotic eccentric. This, he thought, made her a celebrity.

Stein had become such an institution, in fact, that visiting Americans felt deprived if they couldn't meet the Mama of Dada. Since Beach's bookshop served as an unofficial headquarters for visiting American writers and poets, they would "come to me, exactly as if I were a guide from one of the tourist agencies, and beg me to take them to see Gertrude Stein."

One of the first people Beach brought to rue de Fleurus was Sherwood Anderson, whose novel *Winesburg, Ohio* was having a good deal of success. They became immediate fast friends, perhaps because Anderson flattered Stein so shamelessly.

Anderson's wife Tennessee, on the other hand, received the usual treatment reserved for wives: seated on the other side of the room, away from Sherwood and Gertrude, she was forced to chat about housekeeping with Alice. According to Beach, Tennessee tried every possible maneuver to participate in the other conversation, but Alice, whose skillful wife-proofing technique had developed over many years, always managed to head her off.

Anderson introduced Stein to other writers, including, via a letter of introduction, the young unknown Ernest Hemingway. Hemingway in turn brought F. Scott Fitzgerald. The introductions snowballed, and Stein found herself once again besieged by visitors. To hold the tide in check she set visiting hours again, pronouncing herself "at home" most afternoons from 4:30 on.

And so, over the next decade, they came. Some became regular attendees; others came once and never returned—

either because Stein found them "ordinary" and would not invite them back, or because they were bored beyond belief. Some thought Gertrude warm and generous; others found her megalomaniacal and insufferable. The guest list was endless, including, besides those already mentioned, Thornton Wilder, Janet Flanner, Ezra Pound, Margaret Anderson, Juan Gris, Robert McAlmon, Djuna Barnes, William Carlos Williams, Jean Cocteau, Virgil Thomson, George Antheil, Jacques Lipchitz, Ford Madox Ford, and Man Ray.

The large room in which Gertrude held court was comfortably decorated with solid Italian antiques, a bourgeois style belied by the stunning art works covering the walls. The room's centerpiece was Stein herself, enthroned in a well-padded Renaissance chair beneath Picasso's 1906 *Portrait of Gertrude Stein*. From her throne she conducted conversation while Alice served tea, cookies, and cakes (and occasionally strong distilled fruit liqueurs).

But what was it really like? What went on during a salon at 27, rue de Fleurus?

Bravig Imbs, in *Confessions of Another Young Man*, recalled a typical afternoon at Stein's. He arrived first, bringing a gift of bright yellow broom. Next on the scene was Ford Madox Ford. "Gertrude was very fond of him," Imbs wrote, "because he had published excerpts from *The Making of Americans* in the *Transatlantic*." A bit later the painter Pavlik Tchelitchev dropped in, followed by the composer Virgil Thomson who was "dapper as always, and full of chatter." When requested by Gertrude,

Alice reluctantly ceased her conversation with Ford and took her place behind the tea table. It was a sturdy low table, laden with two elaborate silver candlesticks, and a highly wrought silver pot and silver bowl and silver pitcher. The cups and saucers were white, of classic design, ornamented with a heavy gold band.

Sherwood Anderson arrived, a man of such magnetism that he "immediately occupied everyone's attention. . . . Gertrude was captivated by him and wanted to have him all to herself. She sat just opposite him as he gracefully reclined on the sofa, and talked only to him." Picasso was expected but didn't turn up. Just as the party seemed on the verge of breaking up, Juan Gris arrived, "small, dark, with large brooding eyes that could be merry . . . austerely elegant." More tea was passed around and then everybody went home.

Sounds a bit dull, doesn't it? Other writers saw the salon quite differently.

Samuel Putnam:

Inside, we found the walls covered with Picassos. Picasso, Picasso, and more Picasso.

"Yes," Miss Stein informed us, "Picasso has done eighty portraits of me. I sat for that one ninety-one times."

. . . "Your prose, Miss Stein," [Wambly Bald] blurted out, "strikes me as being obscure, deliberately obscure."

At the Salon of Gertrude Stein

The Woman with the Face Like Caesar's never looked more like him than then, as she drew herself up haughtily and replied:

"My prose is obscure only to the lazy-minded. It is a well, a deep well, well it is like a well and that is well."

"There are some people," persisted Wambly, "who are inclined to believe that it is a bottomless well—or one with a false bottom."

At this, Miss Stein's eyes flashed like Caesar's on the field of battle and her voice rang as she answered:

"Naturally, I have my detractors. What genius does not?"

Morrill Cody:

Why this big lump of a woman, this Buddha in a corduroy uniform, should assume such an air of literary authority I could not understand. Nevertheless, I was a little awed by her, impressed in spite of myself. . . . Many of the guests came for the cakes and cookies prepared by Alice, for they were always excellent and satisfying to the hungry bohemians, though the liquid refreshments, except for tea, flowed less generously. Still, as free lunches went, it was pretty good and worth spending an hour listening to the literary exploits and aspirations of Gertrude.

Virgil Thomson:

Having heard in literary circles that George Antheil was that year's genius, [Stein] thought she really ought to look him over. So through Sylvia Beach she asked that he come to call. George, always game but wary, took the liberty . . . of bringing me along for intellectual protection. . . . Naturally I went. Alice Toklas did not on first view care for me, and neither of the ladies found reason for seeing George again. But Gertrude and I got on like Harvard men. As we left, she said to him only good-by, but to me, "We'll be seeing each other."

John Glassco:

The atmosphere was almost ecclesiastical. . . . The room was large and somberly furnished, but the walls held, crushed together, a magnificent collection of paintings—Braques, Matisses, Picassos, and Picabias. I only recovered from their cumulative effect to fall under that of their owner, who was presiding like a Buddha at the far end of the room. . . . Gertrude Stein projected a remarkable power, possibly due to the atmosphere of adulation that surrounded her. . . . She awakened in me a feeling of instinctive hostility coupled with a grudging veneration, as if she were a pagan idol in whom I was unable to believe.

At the Salon of Gertrude Stein

*

The Found Meal for the Salon of Gertrude Stein

LAPSANG SOUCHONG TEA
NAMELESS COOKIES
VISITANDINES
BLACK CURRANT LIQUEUR

———————

The recipes for nameless cookies, visitandines, and black currant liqueur are derived from Alice's personal recipes in *The Alice B. Toklas Cook Book.*

Lapsang Souchong Tea

Lapsang Souchong, with its smoky and mysterious taste, is perhaps the most flavorful of all teas. It seems just the right tea to be prepared by the exotic Miss Toklas.

A discussion on the preparation of tea is contained on page 56 of the Nina Hamnett/Jean Cocteau chapter.

Nameless Cookies

Sift together ¼ cup powdered sugar and 2 cups white flour. Cream 1 cup butter and add the flour mixture slowly, little by little; this procedure, stirring rather than beating as flour is added, should take about 20 minutes. At midway point, add 1 tablespoon curaçao and 1 teaspoon brandy. When mixture has been combined, roll the dough into small "sausage" rolls about 2 inches long and ½ inch thick. Place on lightly oiled cookie sheet 1 inch apart in preheated 275° oven; bake 20 minutes. Remove gently with spatula, gently sifting powdered sugar over them while still hot. Kept in tightly closed container, cookies will last up to 3 weeks.

Visitandines

> Visitandines were first prepared for the Stein/ Toklas household by an early *femme de ménage*, Léonie, who claimed the name derived from the cakes' original inventors, the Visitation order of nuns.

Melt 1¼ cups butter in saucepan until slightly browned. Remove from heat and put aside. In a bowl combine whites of 6 eggs, stirring mixture slowly with wooden spoon. When eggs are thoroughly blended, mix in ⅔ cup sifted white flour until smooth. Add 1 teaspoon vanilla and melted butter, which should now be cool. Fold in 2 stiff, beaten egg whites. Fill lightly buttered muffin tins with mixture and bake in preheated 400° oven until visitandines are golden in color, approximately 20 minutes. Remove and glaze with apricot jam that has been warmed and run through a sieve.

Black Currant Liqueur

Wash and drain thoroughly ½ pound raspberries and 3 pounds black currants; mash. Place in glass or ceramic container, cover with cheesecloth, and put in cool, dark place for 24 hours. At this time add 1 cup clean, dry black currant leaves and 1 quart vodka. Cover bowl again, with a plate this time; let rest another 24 hours. On the third day strain the currant mash through a fine sieve and put momentarily aside. In large saucepan, combine 3 pounds sugar and 3 cups water; bring to boil over low heat and let boil 5 minutes, stirring frequently. Remove from heat and allow to cool completely. When syrup is cool, add to black currant/vodka mixture. Let stand 3 hours, then filter through cheesecloth into bottles. Cork. The liqueur is ready to drink.

1925

In the United States

New book, *Paris on Parade,* states that Paris contains the "interlocking directorate of the advance movement in English letters: Ford, Beach, Joyce, McAlmon, Bird, Hemingway, Antheil and Pound." This sets a new batch of young American writers traveling to Paris to meet literary idols. . . . *The Dove,* a play by Djuna Barnes, opens on Broadway; its star is Judith Anderson . . . Publication of *The Great Gatsby* by F. Scott Fitzgerald; *Manhattan Transfer* by John Dos Passos . . .

In Paris

The Charleston arrives . . . The Hemingways, Harold Loeb, Lady Duff Twysden, Bill Smith, Pat Guthrie, and Donald Ogden Stewart travel to Pamplona, Spain, for the yearly San Fermin Festival; their experience forms basis for Hemingway's first novel, *The Sun Also Rises* . . . 5,000 Americans arrive in Paris each week . . . Death of modern French composer Erik Satie; he leaves huge collection of umbrellas and derby hats . . . Ezra Pound's opera *Testament,* based on poetry of François Villon, performed at the Salle Pleyel; audience and critical reaction favorable

... Kiki arrested in Villefranche on charges of prostitution
... First group exhibition of surrealist painters held in October; Man Ray is only American, others include Picasso, Arp, Ernst, Miro ... Paris World's Fair highlights *les arts décoratifs* (art deco) in architecture and design of furniture, textiles, etc. ... Café Select opens ... Arrivals: Josephine Baker, William Shirer, Elmer Rice, Virgil Thomson (second trip), Brauvig Imbs ... *La Revue Nègre* the hit of Paris ... Première of *Ballet Mécanique* by George Antheil ... First issue of *This Quarter* ... Publication of *The Making of Americans* by Gertrude Stein (Contact Editions) ... Bricktop and Cole Porter meet ...

JOSEPHINE BAKER:
Naked Lunch

The date: October 2, 1925; the place: Théâtre des Champs-Élysées; the show: *La Revue Nègre.* When the curtain rises on opening night, a minor dancer named Josephine Baker is a complete unknown; when it falls, she is the uncontested star of Paris. Rarely in history has a stage appearance created the kind of furor and sensation that Baker's did that night. Her debut had such an impact on journalist Janet Flanner that, writing about it almost fifty years later, the image remained fresh and vivid:

> She made her entry entirely nude except for a pink flamingo feather between her limbs; she was being carried upside down and doing the split on the shoulder of a black giant. Midstage he paused, and with his long fingers holding her basket-wise around the waist, swung her in a slow cartwheel to the stage floor, where she stood, like his magnificent discarded burden, in an instant of complete silence. She was an unforgettable female ebony statue. A scream of salutation spread through the theater. . . . Within a half

hour of the final curtain on opening night, the news and meaning of her arrival had spread by the grapevine up to the cafés on the Champs-Élysées, where the witnesses of her triumph sat over their drinks excitedly repeating their report of what they had just seen.

Not bad for a girl just turned nineteen who could barely read or write. Raised in the St. Louis slums, Baker's early life had nothing in common with the kind of glamour she evinced on the stage. Each winter her stepfather had lined the walls of their one-room apartment with newspapers to keep out the cold. Josephine and her siblings searched garbage cans daily for soup-makings (chicken heads were a prized find). Despite these desperate circumstances, Baker was a happy child with an optimistic outlook on life.

Hoping to better her circumstances, she ran off at the age of thirteen with a black vaudeville troupe called the Dixie Steppers. She played child roles at first, later becoming part of the chorus line. Eventually she landed a dancing job at the Plantation, a popular Harlem nightclub. She stayed there until recruited as a minor dancer in *La Revue Négre*, a black dancing troupe traveling to Paris.

Baker—who would spend the rest of her life in France—loved the country from the first moment, as she recalled in her autobiography, *Josephine*:

We were a wide-eyed, bewildered group, except for Sidney [Bechet, the famed clarinetist] and the

Naked Lunch

dancer Louis Douglas, who had performed in Paris before. Mrs. Caroline and her secretary propelled us toward the wagon-restaurant. In America, Negroes were always told the dining car was full if there were white passengers eating. Here we were smilingly welcomed. We couldn't believe our eyes. "It's like this everywhere," Douglas explained. "Not just in the restaurants. You can buy the best seats in the theater if you like."

The triumphant opening of *La Revue Négre* transformed Josephine's life: almost instantly she had become famous and fawned over. Her every move was reported in the press, her clothes and style were imitated by French women, and cheering crowds formed when she strolled the streets of Paris. When *Revue Négre* moved on, Baker became the star of the Folies-Bergères, which only increased her fame. She sometimes grew tired of the constant attention, comparing herself to a circus animal in fancy dress. When it got to be too much, she'd hide backstage or lock her door and play deaf to the constant knocking. Sometimes the results were amusing:

[One] time the watchman hadn't seen me. Had I perhaps been taken ill in my dressing room? The stage manager rushed off to borrow the firemen's pass key. When they finally opened the door, there I sat, stark naked, calmly eating lobster. Why all the fuss? It didn't take long to put on *my* costume.

Her celebrity status continued to skyrocket. She was dressed, gratis, in creations by Patou and Poiret; she developed a taste for champagne; she painted her fingernails gold, walked a pet leopard named Chiquita through the cobbled streets, and sometimes coiled a pet snake around her neck; she drove an expensive Delage, upholstered in snakeskin, given to her by a wealthy young suitor. Of suitors she had dozens, including one Hungarian who shot himself for love of her. As reported by A. E. Hotchner in *Papa Hemingway*, even strong boys like Ernest Hemingway were not immune to La Baker's charm:

> In the basement of one of these buildings [Hemingway said] was the best night club that ever was—Le Jockey. Best orchestra, best drinks, a wonderful clientele, and the world's most beautiful women. Was in there one night . . . when the place was set on fire by the most sensational woman anybody ever saw. Or ever will. Tall, coffee skin, ebony eyes, legs of paradise, a smile to end all smiles. Very hot night but she was wearing a coat of black fur, her breasts handling the fur like it was silk . . . everything under that silk instantly communicated with me. I introduced myself and asked her name. "Josephine Baker," she said. We danced nonstop for the rest of the night. She never took off her fur coat. Wasn't until the joint closed she told me she had nothing on underneath.

Baker loved her adopted country and proved it during World War II by working for the Resistance, which earned her lieutenant's bars in the French Air Force. She entertained French and Allied troops tirelessly, and was a strong backer of Charles de Gaulle. In time she was awarded both the Legion of Honor with the Rosette of the Resistance and the *croix de guerre.*

Baker was also active in the war against racial prejudice in the United States, giving time and money to organizations such as the NAACP. She refused to entertain in the United States for many years as a protest against discrimination. In 1951 she finally agreed to an American tour, but only in clubs that allowed blacks. Still, she couldn't avoid the insults: reluctantly allowed entry to New York's Stork Club—the first black customer to ever walk through the doors—she was refused service. Sitting in the Stork that night was a young starlet named Grace Kelly. Impressed by Baker's courage, Kelly wondered if she herself would be capable of such bravery.

After the war Baker adopted a dozen orphans and brought them to live in her Dordogne chateau. She called her kids the Rainbow Tribe, and with good reason: their nationalities ranged from Finland to Korea, from the Ivory Coast to Algeria; their religions included Buddhist, Shinto, Moslem, Catholic, and Jewish. She wanted the tribe to serve as an example of world brotherhood. Money was scarce—Baker, never practical, spent everything she made—but the tribe stuck together, and stuck close, even when the chateau was sold at auction to pay debts. Josephine and her tribe squeezed into a three-room apartment in Paris until rescued from their situation by that admiring former starlet, now a princess, who helped them resettle in Monaco.

In 1975, at the age of sixty-eight, Josephine opened in a Golden Anniversary show at the Bobino in Paris. Among those in the sold-out audience were Sophia Loren, Princess Grace, Alain Delon, and Jeanne Moreau. The nine-minute finale called for four costume changes, each more glamorous than the last, culminating in a glittering sheath topped by a three-foot high jeweled and feathered wig. Baker's body was still beautiful, her talent still vibrant: the audience roared its approval in one standing ovation after another. She was mobbed when leaving the theater and toasted until dawn at an elegant dinner for three hundred.

But Baker's heart gave in to the months of exhaustive preparation for this night of glory. She never woke up the next day; by the time her secretary grew alarmed and entered the bedroom, Baker had slipped into a coma. Two days later she was dead.

*

The Found Meal for Josephine Baker

HOMARD GRILLÉ AVEC SAUCE À LA MAÎTRE D'HÔTEL
CHAMPAGNE

Homard Grillé

The recipe for grilled lobster with maître d'hôtel sauce is based on a recipe of Restaurant
Prunier found in the 1926 *Yellow Epicurean
Guide*. Prunier's was the premier seafood
eatery of Paris in the twenties, and very popular with Americans. When Emile Prunier died
in 1925, Janet Flanner paid tribute to him in
her *New Yorker* column, "Genêt," written from
Paris.

In a large kettle make a court boullion. Simmer together
for 15 minutes: 3 cups white wine, 2 cups water, 1 large
onion roughly chopped, 2 stalks celery, 1 carrot chopped,
parsley, a bay leaf, ¼ teaspoon thyme, 6 peppercorns, 1
tablespoon tarragon. Bring to a boil and add 4 live 2-
pound lobsters and steam 15 to 20 minutes.

Remove lobsters; split and clean them, removing
sand sacks in the head and intestinal tubes. Reserve tomalley and coral, rubbing through fine sieve. Dot lobsters
with butter.

Prepare a charcoal fire. Again dot exposed lobster
meat with butter. Grill open side down until slightly

browned, then turn. Dot meat again with butter and grill until warmed through, about 5 minutes. Take care to ensure lobster doesn't get over-heated but only warmed through. Just before serving, spread reserved tomalley and coral on top, add some more butter, and dust with breadcrumbs. Serve alone or with following sauce.

Sauce à la Maître d'Hôtel

Melt ⅓ cup butter in small saucepan; gently stir in ⅓ cup flour and cook resultant roux for 2 to 3 minutes over low heat. Stir in 3 cups chicken stock, ½ teaspoon salt, 2 teaspoons dry mustard, and ¼ teaspoon white pepper and cook over low heat, stirring constantly, until mixture thickens. Continue cooking until reduced to 2 cups. Stir in ½ cup water; when mixture reheats beat in, little by little, ½ cup butter. Add juice of 1 lemon, and fresh chopped parsley and tarragon to taste. Serve hot.

A Few Words About the Champagne . . .

Turn to page 200 for a brief discussion on French champagnes.

Naked Lunch

CONSTANTIN BRANCUSI:

The White Stone Studio

A party chez Brancusi is not to be missed," Margaret Anderson used to say, and few would disagree. Sometimes it seemed that every American in Paris had passed through the anonymous outer portals on the Impasse Ronsin and into the sculptor's geometric, all-white studio. Once there, just about anything could happen; but there was always great food, good wine, and wonderful conversation.

Constantin Brancusi, from a family of Romanian peasants, had come to Paris in 1903 at the age of twenty-seven. He enrolled in the École des Beaux-Arts and by 1907 had embarked on the styles of simplification and primitivism that would mark his work for life. He became widely known in America: in 1913, five of his pieces were shown in the Armory Show; a year later Alfred Stieglitz gave him a one-man exhibition at New York's Gallery of Photo-Secession; in 1921 Margaret Anderson and Jane Heap devoted an entire issue of the *Little Review* to his work; and in 1926 he made headlines around the world when his *Bird in Space* was seized by U.S. customs officials who stated that, since it was not a "recognizable likeness," it was not a work of art and was thus liable for import duty (a lawsuit that made international headlines later decreed that *Bird in Space* was indeed a work of art). By this time Brancusi had become famous worldwide, celebrated everywhere as the first great innovator of modern sculpture.*

Despite fame and fortune, Brancusi's life resembled his sculpture in its simplicity. He never lost touch with his peasant roots, wearing his wooden sabots until the day he died. He usually dressed in overalls, and took great pride in his huge, white beard. After a day's sculpting, he loved nothing better than to entertain friends at home. "*Moi, je déteste les restaurants*," he would say. "*Je mange chez moi, je visite le boucher le matin et j'achète les bifsteaks par le mètre.*"‡

Recollections about Brancusi vary, revealing more about the writer than the sculptor.

Margaret Anderson:

> Constantin Brancusi lives in a stone studio. . . . His hair and beard are white, his long working-man's blouse is white, his stone benches and large round tables are white, the sculptor's dust that covers everything is white, his *Bird* in white marble stands on a high pedestal against the windows, a large white

---

*He's still celebrated. In May 1990 Brancusi's 1928 *Blond Negress*—a golden-hued bronze—was sold for $8.8 million, a record for twentieth-century sculpture as of that date.
‡"I hate restaurants. I eat at home. I go to the butcher in the morning and buy steaks by the yard."

The White Stone Studio

magnolia can always be seen on the white table. At one time he had a white dog and a white rooster. On the stone benches are two cushions, one yellow, the other cerise. . . .

He brings out the violin and plays folk songs with Roumanian abandon and the smile of a child. He sings to you in a soft timid laughing voice. He dances in his heavy sabots. He produces a small drum and makes Duchamp beat it. He dances wildly on the stone floor. Léger sits with his head on one hand and with the other beats the rhythms on the stone table. . . . By seven o'clock in the morning he has led you to the Bois. . . . He suggests taking a boat down the Seine to Rouen. Everyone refuses this. So he takes you instead to the Halles for onion soup.

Kay Boyle:

The next week I went back alone and had lunch of *saucisson* and cheese, and figs, and red wine, with Brancusi under the trees, and helped him plant beans and lettuce along the side of his studio wall.

Caresse Crosby:

My first luncheon with him [Brancusi], à deux, was unforgettable. On his work table he spread a white sheet of crispest tissue paper to serve as tablecloth, in the centre to hold it in place one of his chiselled marble gems. A plump pullet was roasting on the coals, and huge potatoes baking there too. We drank

Rosé from the Midi, and ended the feast with strawberry jam and "hearts of cream." He was a darling, and he cut up the pullet with a sculpting knife. He was in white linen, and I was in black velvet. Together we pulled the wishbone—I don't remember who got the wish.

William Carlos Williams:

. . . went to Brancusi's again, this time for supper, that is for beefsteak cooked by Brancusi himself, the Romanian shepherd, something for which he was famous. We talked, everyone in Paris talked, talked, talked, surrounded by his creations in wood and stone, like the sheep, one might say, cropping out of the chaos of unorganized masses (later to be worked upon), the rocks and trees of a shepherd's world in the flicking half-light about us.

Man Ray:

The first time I went to see the sculptor Brancusi in his studio, I was more impressed than in any cathedral. I was overwhelmed with its whiteness and lightness . . . here and there [was] a roughhewn piece of oak or the golden metallic gleam of a polished dynamic form on a pedestal. . . . A solid white plaster cylinder six feet in diameter, cast on the floor of the studio, served as a table, with a couple of hollowed-out logs to sit on. A few small cushions thrown on these made the seats more inviting.

The White Stone Studio

Nina Hamnett:

He had sculpted a bronze bird that was very beautiful. It was highly polished and shone in the corner of
the studio. The only table was made of white plaster.
It was a solid lump, round, and about four feet in diameter. He asked me to come to dinner with him.
. . . When one dined with him one had to eat and
drink at the same time. He had marvellous burgundy and one started with some apèritifs. As the
evening went on one got into almost a state of coma,
as the "bifsteaks" were certainly measured by metres,
and the Pommard was rather potent.

Robert McAlmon:

Brancusi, a Rumanian peasant with a patriarchal
beard and mild kind eyes, had lately procured a
phonograph and a few records. Brancusi loved
Americans and things American, and pranced about
as the spirit of the jazz age, although at times wearing his wooden *sabots*. Léger and Heyworth and
Cendrars stamped and hooted and catcalled.

*

The Found Meal for Brancusi

KIRSCH
COLD BEANS PURÉE À LA DENIS WITH
GARLIC VINAIGRETTE
GRILLED STEAK
TOMATO AND ANCHOVY SALAD
HEARTS OF CREAM
FRUIT BOWL
WINE

Kirsch

Kirsch is a strong liquor distilled from ripe fermented wild cherries. The finest kirsch comes from the Alsace region of France, but the Black Forest area of Germany also produces its own highly prized version. Serve in small, delicate glasses.

Cold Beans Purée à la Denis

> Brancusi's cold beans purée was mentioned by French writer Pierre Roché in his diary; he called the dish "famous."

Soak 1 cup small white beans overnight in 4 cups water. The next day, simmer beans just until tender, drain, and put through food mill into bowl. Cut 2 slices homestyle white bread; crumble into small bowl and wet with milk. Squeeze out milk and add crumbled bread to beans. Add ½ teaspoon salt and 1 or 2 grinds of pepper. Serve purée on individual plates with generous tablespoon garlic vinaigrette poured atop.

Garlic Vinaigrette

Chop 2 cloves garlic in very fine dice; combine in bowl with ½ to 1 teaspoon Dijon-style mustard and 1 tablespoon red wine vinegar. Slowly add 3 tablespoons high-quality olive oil, beating mixture vigorously with fork all the while. Complete with dash of salt and a few grinds of pepper.

Grilled Steak

Use thick sirloin or porterhouse steaks, ½ pound per person. Lightly wipe steak with paper towel; place on grill 3 to 4 inches above an ashed-over but still-lively bed of coals. Turn once, sprinkling grilled side with salt and pepper. Continue to grill until steak is done, 5 to 10 minutes depending on your taste. When done, remove to warm platter; sprinkle just-cooked side with salt and pepper. Serve at table, cutting meat on the diagonal.

Tomato and Anchovy Salad

Use only the reddest of vine-ripened tomatoes for this salad, 1 per person. Slice tomatoes, remove seeds, and arrange on a serving plate. Sprinkle lightly with salt, freshly ground pepper, and fresh chopped basil. At center, arrange 2 anchovy filets per person. Strew a handful of tiny niçoise olives across the plate; drizzle with highest-quality olive oil and balsamic or red wine vinegar. Serve.

Hearts of Cream

The hearts of cream mentioned here by Caresse Crosby is English for *coeur à la crème*, the dessert described by Langston Hughes. Follow the recipe given on page 121.

Fruit Bowl

Fruit bowls are a common sight in France at the end of a meal, often placed on the table along with a selection of cheeses. Take your prettiest bowl and pile it high with as wide a selection of seasonal fruit as possible. Place the bowl at table's center and give each guest a small plate and a paring knife.

A Few Words About the Wine

Choose a red burgundy for this meal, a Chambertin or Côte de Nuits, for example. You might always want to give wine from Brancusi's native land a try. Romanian wine has a long history; the ancient Greeks traded it through-out the known world, transporting it in amphora. Romanian red wine, which has long afforded U.S. buyers a good value/price ratio, is bold and tasty.

ERNEST HEMINGWAY AND
F. SCOTT FITZGERALD:
Dining Out

I
t was an uneasy friendship from the beginning—
but then, they had so little in common. Scott
Fitzgerald had been educated at Princeton, where
he was a great social success; Hemingway had never been
to college. Fitzgerald spent the war years in stateside mili-
tary bases; Hemingway, an ambulance driver on the Italian front, had been seriously wounded. Fitzgerald was
short; Hemingway tall. Fitzgerald's fair-haired looks were
classic, almost pretty; Hemingway was darkly handsome
and rugged looking. Fitzgerald lacked confidence in his
masculinity; Hemingway portrayed himself as the ultimate tough guy, boasting of his prowess with women and
his feats on both battle- and playing-fields. In Paris,
Fitzgerald and his wife Zelda spent most of their time on
the Right Bank with rich Americans; Hemingway, Hadley,
and their infant son Bumby lived on the Left Bank in vir-
tual poverty. Fitzgerald drank and partied constantly,
writing in fits and starts; each morning without fail Hemingway rose at six to begin his slow, careful day's ration of
work.

When they met, Fitzgerald was at the summit of his popularity; he had produced two collections of short stories, a play, and three novels, the third of which, *The Great Gatsby*, had just been published to solid critical acclaim. Hemingway, on the other hand, had but two slender volumes of short stories to his credit; outside a handful of writers and critics, he was completely unknown. A scant four years later their positions were sharply reversed: Fitzgerald's reputation had begun its steep decline; Hemingway's had taken a jolting ascent with the publication of his first two novels, *The Sun Also Rises* and *A Farewell to Arms*.

Still, to their credit, a friendship *did* develop from their first meeting at the Dingo bar one late April day in 1925. Hemingway remembered talking with some people when he was approached by a man whose face was half-handsome, half-pretty. Fitzgerald introduced himself and praised Hemingway's work. This was a mistake: in Hemingway's code of manly behavior, open praise was akin to insult. Fitzgerald ordered a bottle of champagne, then another; by the end of the second he was quite drunk. A bewildered and slightly disgusted Hemingway put him in a taxi.

They ran into each other a few days later at the Closerie des Lilas. Tense at first, Hemingway relaxed when Fitzgerald remained sober after downing two whiskey-and-sodas. They talked seriously about writing, and then Fitzgerald mentioned that he and Zelda had been forced by bad weather to abandon a car in Lyon. He asked Hemingway to accompany him south on the train to bring the car back to Paris. Hemingway was enthusiastic; it was late spring, an excellent time to travel, and such a trip would give him plenty of time to talk to the more successful writer; he was sure to learn much. Any worries Hemingway might have had after his first encounter with Fitzgerald were eased by the fact that Fitzgerald was now reasonable and charming. And so Hemingway agreed to accompany Fitzgerald to Lyon.

Fitzgerald was to pay for the trip, but when he wasn't at the Gare de Lyon on time, Hemingway bought his own ticket and hopped aboard the train at the last possible minute. In Lyon he took a room and cabled the address to Fitzgerald. Fitzgerald turned up the next morning full of apologies and much the worse for drink. They made peace and left for the drive back to Paris.

At the garage Hemingway was stunned to discover that Zelda had ordered the car's top cut off—she hated being enclosed, Fitzgerald explained, as if the car's destruction made perfect sense. The two men took off in the topless car but were halted by rain an hour north of Lyon; they would be stopped ten times more throughout the day. They drank white Mâcon as they drove along or sheltered beneath plane trees, and soon Fitzgerald was drunk again.

When it began to rain heavily, they took a hotel room, getting into pajamas while their clothes dried beside the fire. Fitzgerald, a hypochondriac even in the best of times, convinced himself he was dying from lung congestion. He crawled into bed where he lay in misery, drinking hot lemonade and whiskey. Who, he worried, would care for Zelda and his daughter Scotty when he was gone? He then proceeded to tell Hemingway intimate details of Zelda's love affair with a French pilot. This kind of revelation disgusted Hemingway, who by now bitterly regretted the entire trip.

Fitzgerald recovered somewhat by the time their clothes were dry and agreed with Hemingway that dinner might help his weakened condition. They dressed and went downstairs. Fitzgerald requested a telephone connection to Zelda in Paris. While waiting, the two men proceeded into the dining room. Fitzgerald was unsteady, but managed to enjoy some snails and a carafe of white wine before his phone call went through. He was gone for about an hour. Hemingway finished the snails.

Finally Fitzgerald returned and ordered chicken. In *A Moveable Feast*, Hemingway recounted what happened next:

> We had eaten very good cold chicken at noon but this was still famous chicken country, so we had poularde de Bresse and a bottle of Montagny, a light, pleasant white wine of the neighborhood. Scott ate very little and sipped at one glass of the wine. He passed out at the table with his head on his hands. It was natural and there was no theater about it and it even looked as though he were careful not to spill nor break things.

A few days after their return to Paris, Fitzgerald gave Hemingway a copy of his just-published *The Great Gatsby*. By now thoroughly disillusioned with Fitzgerald, Hemingway undertook the reading reluctantly. But the book's magic captivated him. If Fitzgerald could write a book as wonderful as *The Great Gatsby*, Hemingway thought, then perhaps he could write one even finer. Hemingway vowed to do everything he could in the future to help Fitzgerald, and to try to be a good friend—no matter how crazy Fitzgerald might become.

And so the friendship, tentative and uneasy as it was, continued.

*

The Found Meal for Ernest Hemingway and F. Scott Fitzgerald

ESCARGOTS À LA BOURGUIGNON
SAUTÉED CHICKEN WITH MORELS
WINE

Escargots à la Bourguignon

Fitzgerald and Hemingway had driven north from Lyon before taking a hotel room, so they were doubtless somewhere in Burgundy. It's a good bet that they were served the traditional snails of the region.

Step 1. Obtain a dozen live snails per person. These can be purchased in many Asian or European markets—they are ready to prepare when purchased, and you may proceed directly to Step 2. You can also find what you need in any garden; however, garden snails must be "purged" before they're edible: keep them in a wire-mesh cage for about 2 weeks, feeding them fresh lettuce and water every day. You may then proceed with the next step.

Step 2. Scrub snails thoroughly but gently. Soak for 48 hours in water to cover, to which has been added ½ cup each vinegar and salt. Drain and replace liquid at least twice during this period.

Step 3. Drain. Plunge snails into pot of boiling court bouillon—2 cups per dozen snails—composed of ½ fish stock and ½ dry white wine, 1 strip of orange peel, 1 teaspoon fennel seeds, 1 tablespoon salt, and a few grinds of fresh pepper. Simmer about 45 minutes. Allow to cool in court bouillon. Remove snails from pan and drain thoroughly. With oyster fork or narrow knife, remove snails from shell. Set snails and shells aside.

Step 4. Prepare sauce. In a bowl, combine 3 cubes softened, unsalted butter, 4 minced shallots, 3 large mashed garlic cloves, 1 tablespoon parsley, 1½ teaspoons salt, and a few grinds of fresh pepper. Blend thoroughly. Let stand at room temperature for at least 1 hour, allowing flavors to blend.

Step 5. Put a little snail butter in each shell, then add a snail and top with more butter. Arrange shells, buttery side up, on a flat pan. Dust lightly with fine, soft bread crumbs. Bake in 400° oven for 5 to 7 minutes, just until they're heated through and bubbling. Serve at once.

Sautéed Chicken with Morels

Chickens raised in Bresse are said to be the best in France—so good, in fact, that they've been the subject of culinary poets for centuries. For this dish buy the finest chicken available, perhaps a variety grown naturally in the outdoors.

Cut a 5-pound chicken into pieces, dividing breast in two. Rinse, dry and dredge in seasoned flour. Set on raised rack and let dry for 10 minutes. When ready, melt 3 to 4 tablespoons butter in a sauté pan. Brown chicken on all sides over slow, low heat, partially covered.

While chicken cooks, carefully clean 1 pound wild, fresh morels or 3 ounces dried (if they're dried, clean out sand and reconstitute with hot water and a bit of brandy; if they're fresh, brush carefully with soft brush to remove sand). Melt 2½ tablespoons butter in small pan; add 1½ teaspoons lemon juice, ½ teaspoon salt, and ¼ cup water, and bring to simmer. Keeping heat very low, add morels; stirring occasionally, continue cooking until juice has almost—but not quite—evaporated.

When chicken is almost done, remove temporarily

from pan and keep warm. Add to pan 1 tablespoon each finely chopped shallots and garlic and sauté over moderate heat. Remove pan from heat; sprinkle 1 teaspoon flour into pan and mix well. Throw in morels and their juice, 3 tablespoons chicken stock or water, and ¼ cup tomato purée. Mix gently and simmer 5 minutes over low heat. Add ½ teaspoon salt, few grinds of pepper, and 1 tablespoon chopped parsley. Return chicken to pan and simmer 10 minutes or until done. Arrange chicken pieces on serving platter, pour morel sauce over, and serve immediately. Garnish with chopped parsley.

A Few Words About the Wine

Fleury, or Fleurie, is sometimes called the queen of Beaujolais wines. Though heavy, it's quite fruity. Serve the Fleury as it was served to Hemingway and Fitzgerald: in a simple glass carafe.

Montagny is, as Hemingway states, a light and pleasant white wine.

BRICKTOP AND COLE PORTER:
Hash and Wine

Bricktop's: the very name evokes a smoky cabaret in jazz-raged Paris, a place for drinking, jiving, jamming, or just letting your hair down late at night—and that's exactly what Bricktop's was. From the start this lively spot attracted not only international high-lifes like Cole Porter and Noël Coward, but the Montparnasse boho set, the ragtime-loving French, and just about any American musician drifting through town.

One reason for Bricktop's success was its intimate feel, from the padded front door with speakeasy peepholes to the illuminated glass dance floor to the banquette-lined walls. Another reason was the music, the most up-to-date jazz in town. The third and most important reason was its owner, Ada Smith, a.k.a. Bricktop.

Charming, lovely, and gracious, Brick could also play tough. In *Being Geniuses Together*, Bob McAlmon recalled sitting in the club one night and watching in amazement as Brick simultaneously added up the day's accounts, sang a lively rendition of "Love for Sale," prevented an angry actress from throwing champagne in her boyfriend's face, and humored a drunken Frenchman into paying his bill. Then, when a fight broke out in the kitchen, she:

> skipped down from her stool, [and] glided across the room, still singing. She jerked aside the curtain and stopped singing long enough to say, "Hey, you guys, get out in the street if you want to fight. This ain't that kind of joint!" Then she continued the song, having missed but two phrases, and was back at her desk again adding accounts.

Bricktop was a light-skinned black woman with freckles and red-gold hair (hence her nickname) who first came to Paris in 1924 for a gig as singer and dancer at Le Grand Duc.* She soon opened her own club, the Music Box, but when it failed she returned to singing. The next year, when Brick decided to give the nightclub business another try, a new friend, Cole Porter, advised her to choose a less jejune name than the last one. He looked surprised when she asked for a suggestion, saying, as if it were obvious, "Bricktop's."

The new club stayed open later than any place in town. People ambled into Brick's at four or five in the morning, able to find companionship, whiskey, champagne, food, and good music. Noël Coward often sat in at the piano. Jascha Heifetz once borrowed the jazz group's violin and played for an hour. A few memorable Sidney Bechet and

---

*Langston Hughes was washing dishes at Le Grand Duc at the same time; interestingly, neither mentions the other in their respective memoirs.

Hash and Wine

Louis Armstrong jam sessions blew on till dawn. Bricktop could name as customers the likes of Scott and Zelda Fitzgerald, Hemingway (whom she disliked), the Prince of Wales, Robert McAlmon, Kay Boyle, Man Ray, Josephine Baker, the Aga Khan, Duke Ellington, Franklin Roosevelt, Jr., Gloria Swanson, Fred Astaire, T. S. Eliot, Fats Waller, Mabel Mercer, and Alberta Hunter.

Cole Porter, who became one of her best friends, introduced her to many whose presence helped make Bricktop's a success. Soon after their 1925 meeting Porter asked Brick if she'd teach the Charleston—popular in America but as yet unknown in France—to the Aga Khan. She was so successful that he asked if she'd try again, this time with the Black Bottom and the Prince of Wales.

In her memoirs Bricktop recalled her first encounter with Porter, which took place at the Music Box:

> One morning in the late fall or early winter of 1925 a slight, immaculately dressed man came in, sat down at one of the tables, and ordered a plate of corned-beef hash with a poached egg on top and a bottle of wine. By morning I mean between three A.M. and six A.M.—we stayed open after the other clubs closed and got quite a few customers during those hours. We only served three things at that time of day— corned-beef hash with a poached egg, creamed chicken on toast, or a club sandwich—but we served them courtesy of the house.
>
> I got up to sing and could sense that the man was

watching and listening with more than ordinary interest. He applauded when I finished the set, I bowed and took up my usual position at the door. He finished eating and got up to leave. Just then Buddy Gilmore came through the door. Buddy was a drummer who'd come to Paris with Vernon and Irene Castle and stayed to form his own group. He grabbed the stranger and started hugging him.

"Who was that?" I asked Buddy later.

"That was Cole Porter," he said.

"Oh, my God!" I said. "I've just been singing one of his songs!"

*

The Found Meal for Cole Porter and Bricktop

CORNED BEEF HASH WITH A POACHED EGG

Corned Beef Hash

The recipe for corned-beef hash is based on Edith Wharton's personal recipe, found in the 1936 book *A Medley of Recipes*. Wharton, author of the great American novels *Ethan Fromme*, *The Age of Innocence*, and *The House of Mirth*, lived in France at the same time as many of the principals in *Found Meals*. However, though she encountered the younger generation on occasion—including one infamous bout of repartee with Scott Fitzgerald, which she won—she remained basically aloof from the twenties expat scene.

Use canned or leftover corned beef. Chop corned beef finely. To 1 part meat, add 1 part cooked, chopped potatoes, a little chopped onion, a little chopped tomato, and pepper and salt to taste. Heat a pan with a little butter, add hash and fry slowly to a nice brown; if dry, moisten with stock or water. Press with spatula and fold in half like an omelet. Press down again.

While the hash is cooking, poach the eggs.

Poached Eggs

Bring 1 quart of water and 1 tablespoon vinegar to boil in a deep saucepan. When almost boiling, lower the heat: water should barely simmer. Break an egg onto a small flat plate and slide the egg gently into the water. Poach until white solidifies, about 3 to 4 minues. Remove from water with slotted spoon to a towel to absorb excess moisture.

Place the egg atop the browned hash. Salt and pepper to taste.

F. SCOTT FITZGERALD AND
SARA MURPHY:
On the Beach

I n the summer of 1925 Cap d'Antibes, a beautiful
village on the French Mediterranean, still held a
simple charm. Telephone service shut down each
day while the operator went home to lunch, and at night
the exchange closed completely. The half-mile beach with
its golden sand was almost always empty. There was a
rather primitive bar, a small café and a movie house that
showed an old film once a week. There was only one small
hotel, and during the summer of 1925 most of its guests
were friends of Gerald and Sara Murphy, whose home,
Villa America, was nearby.

Scott and Zelda Fitzgerald were at Antibes that summer, too, but with typical flamboyance rented a villa of
their own. Scott tried to write, but was more often than
not distracted by the fun and games surrounding the
Murphys. Though Fitzgerald had trouble writing that
summer, his literary imagination wasn't hampered in the
least: much about that season ended up in his fourth and
perhaps greatest novel, *Tender Is the Night.**

---

*Many of the same events would also turn up in Zelda's *Save Me the Waltz.*

Tender revolves around the marriage of Dick and Nicole Diver, a wealthy American couple who live on the Riviera in a home much like the Murphys' Villa America. In fact, much about the Divers is like the Murphys—their lifestyle, their friends, the way they dress, talk, laugh, eat, and entertain. Fitzgerald made no secret about the fact that Dick and Nicole were based on Gerald and Sara; preparing to write the book, he "studied" them openly, subjecting them at times to an almost cruel analysis. Midway through the book, though, the characters do an about-face, becoming more like Zelda and Scott than Gerald and Sara. In the end the lack of character cohesion is the great flaw in *Tender*, but a flaw that pales beside the book's richness, depth, and insight into human tragedy.

Aside from the Murphys, the summer of 1925 provided *Tender Is the Night* with other elements, large and small. First and perhaps most important was Zelda's barely concealed romance with a French aviator, Edouard Jozanne. In *Tender* Jozanne becomes Nicole Diver's daredevil lover, Tommy Barban.

Another borrowed event is Zelda's murder/suicide attempt. One night, while the Fitzgeralds drove along the Grande Corniche high above the Mediterranean, Zelda seized the wheel from Scott and aimed the car at a cliff. At the last second Scott wrenched control and saved their lives; later he worked the experience into *Tender* with a scene in which Nicole attempts to kill herself and Dick in the same fashion.

Lesser borrowings include a celebration at Villa America that became the model for the Divers' famous party; a visiting Englishman, Sir Charles Mendl, who turned up in the book as the homosexual Campion; and Gerald's habit of dressing in a striped sailor jersey to rake seaweed off the beach (in the book's opening scene Dick Diver does the same thing while dressed in the same way).

And then there was Sara/Nicole. "I used you again and again in *Tender*," Fitzgerald wrote Sara Murphy years later. "I tried to evoke not *you* but the effect that you produce on men—the echoes and reverberations—a poor return for what you have given by your living presence."

Fitzgerald's crush on Sara was an open secret. His behavior was usually more subdued when she was around, and there were often times he couldn't keep from gazing at her like a dazzled college freshman. At *Tender*'s beginning, before the Nicole Diver character becomes too troubled and turns into Zelda Fitzgerald, she is Sara Murphy right down to her long string of pearls. Sara was famous for those pearls; she wore them constantly, even to the beach, where she slung them down her back, saying the sun was good for them. This throwaway gesture fascinated the Murphys' friend Picasso, whose paintings of the period often show women frolicking on the sand with long strings of pearls across their backs.

Here is Sara/Nicole as she was seen by Scott Fitzgerald in *Tender Is the Night*.

Nicole Diver, her brown back hanging from her pearls, was looking through a recipe book for

On the Beach

chicken Maryland. She was about twenty-four, Rosemary guessed—her face could have been described in terms of conventional prettiness, but the effect was that it had been made first on the heroic scale with strong structure and marking, as if the features and vividness of brow and coloring, everything we associate with temperment and character, had been molded with a Rodinesque intention, and then chiseled away in the direction of prettiness to a point where a single slip would have irreparably diminished its force and quality. With the mouth the sculptor had taken desperate chances—it was the cupid's bow of a magazine cover, yet it shared the distinction of the rest.

*

The Found Meal for Scott Fitzgerald and Sara Murphy

CHICKEN MARYLAND
TOMATOES PROVENÇALE
FRESH CORN OFF THE COB

Thanks to John Dos Passos for the addition of corn and tomatoes: "One of Sara's favorite dishes," he wrote, "was . . . Golden Bantam corn cut off the cob and sprinkled with paprika; homegrown tomatoes cooked in olive oil and garlic on the side. Sometimes to this day when I'm eating corn on the cob I recapture the flavor, and the blue flare of the Mediterranean noon, and the taste of vin de Cassis in the briney Mediterranean breeze."

Chicken Maryland

Another popular twenties recipe: according to Janet Flanner, Chicken Maryland was Natalie Barney's favorite dish. This recipe is loosely derived from one that appeared in a 1930 edition of *The Joy of Cooking*.

Cut a 3½ pound chicken into pieces. Dip each piece into milk, season with salt and pepper, dredge in flour, and let dry 30 minutes. In heavy skillet heat 3 tablespoons vegetable oil and sauté chicken on all sides until nicely browned. Add 1 cup hot water, ¼ teaspoon cumin, and ¼ teaspoon sage, and let come to boil. Immediately reduce heat, cover, and let simmer 45 minutes. Remove lid and simmer until all moisture has evaporated from pan. Serve.

Tomatoes Provençale

Cut 4 large tomatoes in half through stem; remove seeds; salt and pepper tomatoes. Sauté, cut side down, in 3 tablespoons hot olive oil, approximately 5 minutes or until juices have evaporated. Turn onto rounded sides and sauté another 2 minutes. Place cut side up in baking dish.

In separate skillet, sauté 2 large cloves finely chopped garlic in 2 tablespoons olive oil until garlic is lightly browned. Spoon sauce evenly over tomatoes and slide baking dish beneath preheated broiler for 3 to 4 minutes, until tomatoes are browned on top.

Fresh Corn off the Cob

Cut corn from 4 cobs with a knife (this goes easier if you hold the cob upright in a large flat pan; in this way the cut corn and juices are easily collected. When you're through scraping off the corn go over the cob again with the back side of the knife, pressing hard to release remaining juices and kernels).

Simmer the cut corn in its own juices 2 to 3 minutes, then add ½ tablespoon butter, salt and white pepper to taste, and ¼ cup of cream. Continue cooking another minute or so and then transfer to warm serving bowl. Sprinkle lightly with paprika and serve.

1926

In the United States

Sinclair Lewis refuses the Pulitzer Prize . . . Martha Graham makes New York debut as dancer and choreographer . . . publication of *The Sun Also Rises* by Ernest Hemingway; *White Buildings* by Hart Crane; *The Weary Blues* by Langston Hughes; *The Cubical City* by Janet Flanner . . .

In Paris

Franc now fifty to the dollar; an average three-course meal in Paris costs the equivalent of twenty cents . . . Art inflation note: Rousseau's *The Sleeping Bohemian,* for which he was paid 400 francs, is auctioned at Drouet's for half a million francs . . . Over the summer 109 passenger ships bring visitors to Le Havre or Cherbourg from New York . . . Arrival: Isadora Duncan . . . Gertrude Stein and Natalie Barney meet for the first time, though both have lived in Paris since the turn of the century . . . Publication of *Palimpsest* by H.D. . . . . Composition of *Sonata da Chiesa* by Virgil Thomson . . . Bricktop's opens . . . Claude Monet dies at Giverney . . .

Caviar Enough?

I sadora Duncan challenged from adolescence the strictures of nineteenth-century morality and complacence. Her first shocking appearance on the stage—leaping about half-nude, barefoot, and uncorseted in flowing Greek robes—forever liberated women from whalebone and petticoats. Early in her career she was denounced by the clergy for baring her legs onstage; years later, she was banned in Boston for exposing her breasts. She espoused the concept of free love, refusing to marry until, in her early forties, she wed a mad Russian poet seventeen years her junior. She not only believed in but practiced polyandry (each of her three children had a different father),* and she legally adopted and supported many other children throughout her lifetime. She was a political liberal, consistently championing the underdog and supporting revolutions in Russia, Spain, and Greece.

There was nothing modest about Isadora; everything she did or felt was done and felt lavishly—her dance, her

---

*Two of her children died in an automobile accident, a tragedy from which she never quite recovered. The third child died at birth.

gestures, her speech, her love affairs, her politics. She was wildly impractical. Once in New York she spent her last two thousand dollars on flowers; the next day, broke, she was unable to buy a steamship ticket back to Europe. Another time she gave a party that started in Paris, moved on to Venice, and finally ended on a houseboat in the Nile. Even at her poorest, she insisted on drinking the best champagne every night.

At one time Isadora was probably the most famous woman on earth. When she performed in Tokyo, London, Buenos Aires, Moscow, or Warsaw, audiences wept in adulation. Music and conversation stopped abruptly when she entered a restaurant, the eyes of customers, musicians, and waiters following her progress across the floor. She was pursued by millionaires and princes. Rodin chased her across Europe, sketching her endlessly. Emile-Antoine Bourdelle used her as the main figure in his frescoes in the Théâtre des Champs-Élysées. Her intimates were the day's megastars: Sarah Bernhardt, Eleanora Duse, Leon Bakst, Anatole France, Ellen Terry (whose son, the stage designer Gordon Craig, was the father of Duncan's first child).

In the early twenties, Duncan accepted a Bolshevik invitation to live in Russia and establish a dancing school in Moscow. Three years later, disillusioned with the class system developing under Communism, she returned to Europe with her new (and only) husband, the poet Serge Esenin. The marriage had problems from the start: not only did neither speak the other's language, but their mutually heavy drinking resulted in violence and constant public scenes. Esenin eventually returned to Russia, where he hanged himself two years later.

Isadora came to live in Paris in 1926. Though she had made and spent many fortunes in her life, she was now nearly penniless, forced to take an inexpensive suite of rooms in Montparnasse. Across the street was the Dingo, and nearby were the Rotonde, the Dôme, and the Select. Jimmie the Barman, who was tending the Parnasse Bar on the bottom floor of her apartment building, saw her practically every day. He considered her a good drinker, someone who drank steadily but didn't get sloppy. In fact, he said, drinking served only to make her happier.

Isadora gave frequent parties at which just about everyone—politicians, musicians, artists, members of the communist party, journalists, and socialites—was welcome. Late at night, usually accompanied on the piano by the renowned Russian pianist Victor Seroff, she danced barefoot for her guests. In her late forties and heavier now, she no longer moved like a graceful sylph, yet she still had the power to captivate a young man of twenty-two named William Shirer. In the first volume of his memoirs, *20th Century Journey: The Start*, he wrote:

> Some time after midnight the talking and the drinking would subside, the young Russian pianist would sit himself at the piano, and Isadora would dance. I sat on the floor entranced. I had never before seen such natural, graceful, rhythmic movements of a human body. They seemed to flow harmoniously

Caviar Enough?

out of some intense inner fire ... her dancing was still a magnificent thing. Invariably her last dance would be the carmagnole, her tribute to the French Revolution, in which she glided across the room trailing a bright-red scarf—the scarf that in the end would kill her.

Duncan had always given generously to others and now, when she had nothing left to give, her admirers indulged her as they could. Someone always materialized to pay for the pile of saucers sitting before her in a café, or to take her on a trip to the south, or to buy an expensive meal at Prunier's. One of her benefactors was the poet and playwright Mercedes de Acosta,* who, in *Here Lies the Heart*, wrote:

> One day she [Isadora] jokingly complained that no one ever gave her enough caviar, strawberries, asparagus, or champagne. These were the four treats she said she loved the most. So a few days later I invited her to my flat. In the middle of the table were seven great piles of asparagus, already cooked, and surrounded by pyramids of caviar. Circling this was an array of bottles—only the best champagne—and at the four corners of the table were baskets of freshly picked strawberries. Placed around the room on every flat surface were mounds of asparagus, strawberries, and caviar, and more bottles of cham-

---

*De Acosta is rumored to have been the lover of Greta Garbo.

pagne. Isadora was enchanted. When she left that night I gave her all that was left of the feast to take home.

One would almost *expect* Isadora to die extravagantly —and she did. While staying on the Riviera, she talked an automobile dealer into giving her a test-drive of a low-slung Bugatti racer, a car she couldn't possibly afford to buy. Her friends gathered around as she settled into the passenger seat; it was early fall, and the night held a slight chill, so she wrapped a long red scarf around her neck and flung it backward. No one noticed that the car had no fenders or that the spoked rear wheels rose to her shoulders.

"*Adieu, mes amis,*" Isadora sang out. "*Je vais à la gloire!*"

The driver started the powerful engine with a roar and the car leaped forward. Isadora's fringed scarf caught in the spokes, pulled her backward, and broke her neck. She died instantly.

*

The Found Meal for Isadora Duncan

CAVIAR
COLD ASPARAGUS WITH SAUCE RAVIGOTE
STRAWBERRIES
CHAMPAGNE

Simplicity here: this is finger food, and, other than a spoon for the caviar, there is no need for cutlery.

Cold Asparagus

Plan on 10 fat or 20 thin spears per person. Asparagus needs peeling only if it's thicker than a pencil. To peel, hold a spear firmly and, starting near the tip, remove outer skin with a small knife or peeler. Peeling near the tip should be shallow, increasing in thickness at the root end. Break or cut off tough and woody part of stem; wash peeled spears in cold water. Tie into bundles about 4 inches thick.

Bring salted water to boil in pan large enough to hold bundles vertically. When boil is reached, insert bundles and reduce heat; cook uncovered for 5 to 10 minutes depending on thickness of spears. Asparagus is done when a sharp knife easily pierces root end. Plunge immediately into a basin of cold water to stop cooking and maintain a beautiful green color. Remove from water to a towel to drain and cool further. Arrange on serving dish. Serve with Sauce Ravigote.

Sauce Ravigote

To the basic recipe for Sauce Vinaigrette (see page 185), add the following: 2 scant teaspoons chopped capers, 1 teaspoon minced shallot, 2 tablespoons chopped fresh parsley.

Strawberries

Isadora doubtless ate *fraises de bois*, the wild, tiny strawberries easily available in French markets. They're not so easy to find in the United States, however; so unless you live in the woods near a thriving patch of wild strawberries, you'll have to make do with what you find in the market. Choose the ripest, smallest strawberries you can find. Wash in cold water and let dry on paper towels—don't remove the stem! Arrange in a pretty bowl. They need no accompaniment except, perhaps, a small side dish of brown sugar for dipping.

Champagne and Caviar

For a discussion on how to purchase and serve champagne and caviar refer to page 198.

Caviar Enough?

ERNEST HEMINGWAY II:

Dinner at the Rendezvous-des-Mariniers

*E*rnest Hemingway's first novel, *The Sun Also Rises*, is one of the most famous romans à clef of all time. The book's publication in 1926 made instant legends of its thinly disguised, somewhat tragic characters, most of whom could be seen until the late twenties drinking and carousing in the very bars described in the novel. These people have by now become intertwined with his life: it's hard to find a biography of Hemingway that doesn't speculate on his relationship with Harold Loeb, the model for Robert Cohn in the novel, or display a photograph of the androgynously beautiful Duff Twysden (Lady Brett); though famous as a humorist in his day, most people now remember Donald Ogden Stewart because he, along with Hemingway's childhood friend Bill Smith, served as a model for Bill Gorton, one of *Sun's* few sympathetic characters.

Needless to say, the book created a sensation in Montparnasse, home to both author and characters. Janet Flanner, writing in one of her fortnightly columns in *The New Yorker*, revealed that the book's publication had jarred the usually unflappable Montparnassians—especially its easily identified leading characters: "The titled British declassée and her Scottish friend, the American Frances and her unlucky Robert Cohn with his art magazine . . . all these personages are . . . to be seen just where Hemingway so often placed them at the Select."

Not everyone was pleased. Hemingway, in a conversation years later with A. E. Hotchner, recalled that the day after *Sun* was published, he "got word that Harold Loeb, who was the Robert Cohn of the book, had announced that he would kill me on sight." In his memoirs Jimmie the Barman recalled the fury of the novel's real-life counterparts; all Montparnasse, he said, laughed about "six characters in search of an author . . . with a gun!"

But the characters weren't the only real-life aspect of *Sun*: all of expatriate Paris lay in its pages. There were the bars and bistros, the dancing spots and sidewalk cafés, the walks along the quais; there were drinks at the Hotel Crillon, taxis lumbering down the Boulevard Raspail, chestnut trees in bloom in the Luxembourg Gardens. There was also a dinner in a simple hotel/restaurant on the Ile St. Louis, the Rendezvous-des-Mariniers—a dinner that may well be the most famous meal of the decade.

Owned and managed by the amiable Madame Le Comte, the Rendezvous was well known among the literary set long before Hemingway wrote about it, appreciated for its zinc bar, small marble-topped tables, and view of the beautiful old houses on the quai. Dos Passos took a room there in 1919 while studying at the Sorbonne and writing his first novel. Sherwood Anderson ate there on his first visit to Paris in 1921, and Harry Crosby mentioned the Rendezvous frequently in his diaries. Next door, working from an ancient wine cellar, Ford Madox Ford edited the *Transatlantic Review* (Hemingway, an unpaid assistant, frequently sat on the nearby quai editing manuscripts). Sharing the same space were William Bird's Three Mountains Press and Robert McAlmon's Contact Editions. The restaurant—with its very good food and modest prices—thus became a popular meeting place for editors and writers.* In fact, with the exception of Trianons, no restaurant is mentioned so often in contemporary American accounts.

The Rendezvous is gone now, its place long since taken by another restaurant. It is chiefly remembered for its presence in *The Sun Also Rises*: Jake Barnes (loosely based on Hemingway himself) and his pal Bill Gorton enjoy a good meal at Madame Le Comte's and then take a walk around the island. Today, almost seventy-five years later, you can still see Americans, a copy of *Sun* in hand, tracing their footsteps.

> We ate dinner at Madame Lecomte's restaurant on the far side of the island. . . . Bill had eaten at the restaurant in 1918, and right after the armistice, and Madame Lecomte made a great fuss over seeing him. . . .

---

*Musicians, too: in his memoirs, Virgil Thomson mentions dining there regularly.

We had a good meal, a roast chicken, new green beans, mashed potatoes, a salad, and some apple-pie and cheese. . . .

After the coffee and a *fine* we got the bill, chalked up the same as ever on a slate, that was doubtless one of the 'quaint' features, paid it, shook hands, and went out. . . .

We walked along under the trees that grew out over the river on the Quai d'Orléans side of the island. Across the river were the broken walls of old houses that were being torn down. . . .

We walked on and circled the island. The river was dark and a bateau mouche went by, all bright with lights, going fast and quiet up and out of sight under the bridge. Down the river was Notre Dame squatting against the night sky. We crossed to the left bank of the Seine by the wooden footbridge from the Quai de Béthune, and stopped on the bridge and looked down the river at Notre Dame. Standing on the bridge the island looked dark, the houses were high against the sky, and the trees were shadows.

"It's pretty grand," Bill said. "God, I love to get back."

*

Dinner at the Rendezvous-des-Mariniers

The Found Meal for Ernest Hemingway

ROAST CHICKEN
MASHED POTATOES
NEW GREEN BEANS
GREEN SALAD
APPLE TART AND CHEESE
COFFEE
FINE

Roast Chicken

Take a 4-pound roasting chicken, rinse and dry thoroughly. Season cavity with salt and pepper, and truss legs and wings. Place chicken on rack in roasting pan, breast side up. Rub skin with 1 tablespoon butter; season with salt. Add ¼ cup water to pan and place uncovered in hot oven (425°); after 15 minutes turn chicken breast side down. Continue turning every 15 minutes, basting with juices collected in pan. When chicken begins to take on color, reduce heat to 375°. Continue turning and basting; add more water if necessary, just enough to keep juices from drying up. After about 1½ hours, pierce thigh with fork; if juices run clear, chicken is done. Remove from pan to warmed platter and let rest for 10 minutes before serving.

Pour off all but a teaspoon of fat from roasting pan. Add 1 teaspoon flour and cook on top of stove over medium heat for 2 to 3 mintues. Slowly add 1 cup hot water or stock to pan juices, scraping up crusty brown bits; cook 3 to 4 minutes. Add salt and fresh-ground white pepper to taste; swirl in a tablespoon of butter. Serve with chicken.

Mashed Potatoes

Peel and quarter 2 pounds medium-sized potatoes; place in large pan and cover with salted water. Bring to boil and cook until soft. Drain potatoes, put through a ricer or purée with masher. Return mixture to pan and stir with wooden spoon until smooth. Add salt and pepper to taste, 3 tablespoons butter, and gradually stir in over low heat approximately ⅓ cup hot milk (or cream) to obtain desired consistency. Beat potatoes until fluffy. Cover and serve immediately.

New Green Beans

Some U.S. markets carry haricots verts, which are far more slender than the average American green bean. If you can't find haricots verts, choose the smallest green beans available.

Trim and wash 1½ pounds fresh, firm green beans. Bring large pot of lightly salted water to boil and then, a handful at a time, drop beans into water. Return water to boil and reduce heat, cooking beans slowly for approximately 5 minutes. Test by tasting: the beans should be tender but still retain crispness. Drain. Toss with 2 tablespoons of butter and serve.

Green Salad

Use one or more fresh and impeccable greens such as endive, cress, romaine, bibb, butter, arugula, dandelions, and nasturtium; a few leaves of radicchio; perhaps a sprinkling of chopped chervil or chives. Wash in cold water and dry thoroughly. Tear greens into bite-sized pieces and chill until ready to serve. At the last moment toss with vinaigrette sauce.

Vinaigrette Sauce

Combine in bowl 1 tablespoon red wine vinegar, 3 tablespoons excellent olive oil, ½ teaspoon Dijon mustard; beat lightly with fork or wire whip for 30 seconds. Season with salt and pepper to taste.

Apple Tart

> Apple pie and cheese are a solely American treat, virtually unavailable in France. Jake and Bill most likely had a cheese course followed by an apple tart.

For the tart pastry, use the recipe given for raspberry and strawberry tarts in the Natalie Barney chapter, page 96. When pastry has been removed from the refrigerator, roll it out to ¼ inch rather than ⅛ inch, pressing evenly into lightly buttered tart pan. Flute rim with fork tines.

Core, peel, and cut into ⅛-inch slices 4 cups firm cooking apples—Goldens, Winesaps, or Rome Beauties, for example. Place in mixing bowl, tossing gently with 1 tablespoon lemon juice, 2 tablespoons sugar, and 2 tablespoons Calvados or brandy. Arrange slices in tart shell, overlapping neatly in a circular pattern. Sprinkle lightly overall with sugar and bake in a preheated 350° oven for 25 to 35 minutes until crust is golden brown.

Fine

The word *fine* is shorthand for Grand Fine Champagne, a blend of spirits from the two highest-quality growing areas of Cognac, Grande Champagne and Petite Champagne. Fine is thus an excellent cognac.

TOUT LE MONDE:

Welsh Rarebit at the Select

The streets of Montparnasse supported dozens of cafés in the twenties, but none more popular than the Dôme, the Rotonde, and the Select. By merely crossing the street from one to the other you could dramatically change the tempo and mood of your day. Large, noisy groups congregated at the Dôme, pushing tables together and taking boisterous command of the sidewalk. The Rotonde—one-time hangout of exiled Bolsheviks—was geared toward quiet, intimate conversation; here one could hold a long and serious discussion on the demise of dadaism or speculate endlessly about what was really wrong with America.

And the Select? Well, some might call it picturesque, some scruffy, others just plain squalid. In *The Confessions of a Harvard Man*, the writer Harold Stearns, who was practically a permanent resident,* called it "a seething mad-house of drunks, semi-drunks, quarter drunks, and sober maniacs."

---

*Stearns served as the model for Harvey Stone in *The Sun Also Rises*. Hemingway places him outside the Select, a pile of saucers piled before him, cadging drinks from passersby.

The café's owners, whose real name was Jalbert, were never called anything but M. and Mme. Select by their customers. M. Select, an amiable enough fellow with twirling mustaches, stayed behind the bar; one rarely reads anything about him. The memoirs are invariably reserved for the formidable guardian of the cash register, Mme. Select. Heavy of bosom, with fingerless gloves and a scowling, watchful demeanor, her evenings were not complete without an impassioned altercation. Robert McAlmon swore that she thrived on battle and never gave a drink "to anybody who did not give her a snappy argument."

The cantankerous Mme. Select was rumored to be a police spy because she called the police at the slightest provocation. The most memorable occasion involved the poet Hart Crane. One night, drinking Cutty Sark, Crane amassed an enormous pile of saucers. Finally the waiter asked him to pay. Crane announced that he had no money. Mme. Select stepped in screaming, and the battle was on! Eventually Mme. Select called *les flics*, but before they arrived, Crane decked four waiters. When a solitary policeman charged into the café, Crane slugged him too. Reinforcements were called in and Crane was dragged feet first from the café by a bevy of cops, his head banging against the cobblestoned street. He spent the next three weeks in prison.

The main reason for the Select's popularity was that it stayed open all night: no matter what hour you dragged back to Montparnasse from a night on the town, you could find warmth, companionship, and something to drink at the Select. You could find something to eat, too, since it had a tiny but always available menu. Its chief offering was Welsh rarebit, usually prepared by M. Select on a little stove behind the bar.

Sometimes a Select rarebit became irretrievably connected with life's bigger moments. John Glassco recalled his first evening at a fancy house—Mme. Hibou's in Montmartre—to which he went with his friends Sidney Schooner and Graeme Taylor. Afterward, walking through the streets:

> How happy and peaceful I felt! Schooner was looking at his watch. 'We've just time to catch the Metro back to the quarter," he said. "How about a Welsh rarebit at the Select?"

A rarebit could also be the occasion of high drama. As Canadian writer Morley Callaghan recalled in his book, *That Summer in Paris*, he and his wife were drinking at the Select with Robert McAlmon when:

> McAlmon, exhilarated by our debate, and getting tight, had become truly expansive. He ordered another champagne cocktail and a Welsh rarebit. When the waiter brought the rarebit McAlmon tasted it, and dropped his fork. "Tell Madame Select," he said in a disgusted tone, "that this rarebit did not come from the kitchen. It came from the toilet." The waiter hurried to Madame Select . . .

Approaching our table, quivering with rage, she told McAlmon she, herself, had made the rarebit. In that case, said McAlmon, waving his hand disdainfully, she ought to know where it came from.

✶

The Found Meal for The Select

WELSH RAREBIT

Welsh Rarebit

> This rarebit is based on a personal recipe of Charlie Chaplin, discovered in *Sincerely Yours: A Collection of Favorite Recipes of Well-Known Persons*, published in 1942.

Melt ½ pound grated cheddar cheese and ½ cup warm ale or beer in top of double boiler placed over boiling water. When cheese melts, add 2½ tablespoons butter and blend thoroughly with spoon. Add 1 teaspoon Worcestershire, ¼ teaspoon dry mustard, and healthy dash cayenne pepper. Continue to heat slowly; when mixture begins to bubble, remove from heat and spoon over buttered toast triangles. Serve.

Welsh Rarebit at the Select

1927

In the United States

George Antheil conducts *Ballet Mécanique* in New York; receives hostile, mocking reception ... Publication of *Men Without Women* by Ernest Hemingway ...

In Paris

Alexander Calder arrives wearing an orange-and-yellow plaid suit; in the fall he sells his first wire sculpture (of Josephine Baker). Other arrivals: Waverley Root, George Orwell, A. J. Liebling, William Carlos Williams (second trip), John Glassco, Samuel Putnam ... Elliot Paul and Eugène Jolas publish first issue of *Transition* ... Charles Lindbergh lands the *Spirit of St. Louis* at Le Bourget outside Paris, May 21; 100,000 Frenchmen and exiled Americans are on the field to greet him when he lands ... Death of Isadora Duncan ... Exhibition of Kiki's art called most successful opening of the year ... *Paris Tribune* reporters William Shirer and Waverley Root look on while angry mob attempts break-in of U.S. Embassy following executions of Sacco and Vanzetti ... Grand opening of Le

Coupole on December 20 with complimentary glass of champagne; another instant success . . . First issue of Ezra Pound's *The Exile* published in Dijon . . . Gerald Murphy paints *Wasp and Pear* . . . "I Can't Give You Anything But Love" most popular song in Paris . . .

HARRY AND CARESSE CROSBY:

Pompeiian Nights

H arry and Caresse Crosby would be splendid subjects for a debate. Their life together was one of
such wild contradiction that no matter the
point made by one team, the other could easily provide an
opposing point of view:

Team A: They were flamboyant, decadent, and extravagant. They threw nightly orgies in their apartment, drank
like fish, fried their brains with opium and hashish, and
sauntered through the streets of Paris with a whippet on a
jeweled leash.

Team B: They were dedicated poets and publishers. In
the five years between the startup of their Black Sun Press
and Harry's suicide, they produced thirty-four beautifully
printed, high-quality books—and half of those were their
own writings, mostly poetry.

Team A: They were second-rate poets!

Team B: Ah, but they were first-rate publishers—*and*
they left a top-quality history, through their second-rate
poems, of the underside of intellectual life in the Paris of
the twenties.

Team A: Bob McAlmon, who was no slouch in the

drinking and degeneracy department, despised them for their decadence and profligate alcoholism.

Team B: He despised everybody! Now take someone like the prim and proper Sylvia Beach. *She* said the Crosbys were the most charming people she'd ever met. So there!

Harry Crosby—a nephew of tycoon J. P. Morgan and a descendant of Alexander Hamilton—was born into Boston's wealthy social elite. In 1917, at the age of nineteen, he volunteered for the American Field Service Ambulance Corps and sailed for France, where he participated in the Battle of Verdun and was awarded a *Croix de Guerre* for heroism. During battle a shell fell on his ambulance, destroying everything but the portion in which he sat. Some historians claim that this experience—whose anniversary Harry observed every year thereafter—was the beginning of his long obsession with death.

At war's end Crosby returned home to attend Harvard University. He soon met and fell in love with Mary Peabody, nicknamed Polly, whose marriage to an alcoholic businessman was rapidly falling apart. Polly, from an old and wealthy family herself, was a descendant of steamboat inventor Robert Fulton.* Despite heavy opposition from both families, Polly divorced her husband and married Harry. In 1922 they took up residence in Paris on the Ile St. Louis.

---

*Polly herself was an inventor: her design for a wireless brassiere was patented in 1914 and later sold to Warner Brothers Corset Company for $15,000.

Pompeiian Nights

For a year Harry worked for his uncle Morgan's bank, but his heart wasn't in it. He preferred to play. At first he and Polly gambled heavily, buying race horses and racing dogs. When this grew tiring, they began writing poetry. Eventually, after they decided to devote their lives to writing, Harry quit his job.

The simplest way to get their work published was to become publishers, and so they did, establishing in 1924 the Black Sun Press. It was around this time that Polly decided to change her name to something less mundane and more poetic. Harry insisted the name chosen be able to form a cross with his, and they eventually settled on Caresse. The Crosby Cross, which appeared in many of their books, thus came into being:

```
          C
          A
    H A R R Y
          E
          S
          S
          E
```

Aside from their own work, the Crosbys published D. H. Lawrence, Archibald MacLeish, Kay Boyle, James Joyce, Hart Crane, Marcel Proust, Henry James, and Ezra Pound. They found a master printer who turned their ideas about design into reality, and Black Sun books are still notable today for their elegance and quality.

Harry's obsession with death intensified, combining with an almost pagan worship of the sun, the symbol of daily death and rebirth. On a trip to Egypt he had a sun tattooed on his back. He wrote poems to the sun and wore a ring with a sun symbol reputed to have come from the tomb of Tutankhamen. His published diaries are rife with references to the sun-goddess, targets pierced by the arrows of the sun, Bokhara sunfire, sun tower, sunstroke, and the sun as a witch's cauldron. Some passages are exuberant:

> It is NOON My Fire Arrows into the Sun Ra Ra Ra Ra
> I PENETRATE INTO THE SUN
> I AM THE SUN.

Others are suicidal. In a poem entitled "Sun Death," he lists famous suicides and writes of achieving an orgasm with the slave-girl of death. In another poem, "Assassin," he speaks of murdering himself by cutting out his own heart and walking with it toward the sun. Harry's death wish eventually played out in New York City on December 10, 1929, in a murder/suicide pact with his current lover, Josephine Rotch.

But back in Paris, despite their commitment to Black Sun, the Crosbys led a fabulous social life. They leased an old mill outside Paris, once home to the philosopher Jean Jacques Rousseau, and transformed it into a country residence suitable for extravagant entertainment. They often

Pompeiian Nights

hosted art students for dinner, and were in turn invited to the students' Quatz Arts Ball, a yearly Parisian bacchanalia.

Before the ball the Crosbys held a champagne dinner and then everybody—Caresse with bosom bared atop a baby elephant—marched through the streets. Harry's costume consisted solely of a dead-pigeon collar and a strategically placed bag of snakes. Later in the evening a naked Caresse was the centerpiece of the students' float, which won first prize. Caresse and Harry left separately with different partners, and she found him hours later sharing their sunken marble bathtub with three beautiful women.

As a matter of fact, the Crosbys often bathed and slept *en masse*, as Caresse herself confessed:

When we wanted to be entertained we received in bed. . . . We always drank champagne and we almost always began with caviar. Our guests were invited to take baths if they wanted to, for we had a sunken marble tub in a black and white tiled bathroom that boasted a white bearskin rug and an open fireplace, as well as a cushioned chaise lounge covered in rose red towelling. We liked to experiment in bath oils and bath salts. There was a great quantity of them to play with and most of our friends lived in Latin Quarter rooms where the plumbing was kept a dark secret. Chez nous martinis and rose geranium mingled in libation. We also provided voluminous bathrobes. Some evenings were rather Pompeiian. The bath could hold four.

*

The Found Meal for Caresse and Harry Crosby

CAVIAR

CHAMPAGNE

A Few Words About Caviar . . .

Buying Caviar. Only sturgeon produce the roe known as caviar. Until recently, almost all the world's caviar came from sturgeon of the Caspian Sea. However, American domestic sturgeon—and its roe—is making a comeback. While not quite as good as that from the Caspian Sea, American caviar is a great deal less expensive. The color and size of caviar varies depending on the type.

American Black: American black is usually about the size of a small caper; as its name implies, it's black in color.

Caspian: Three varieties are available in the United States. Beluga, the most well known, is also the largest and softest, its color steel-gray to black. Osetrova is smaller, firmer, and less expensive than beluga; its color is gray-green to brown. Sevruga is the smallest, firmest, and least expensive; its color is gray-black.

If you can, buy fresh caviar, which comes prepared in two ways, malossol or pressed. Malossol means "lightly salted"; the tiny amount of salt helps keep the eggs fresh. Only the very highest quality eggs are used in this process. They will thus be perfectly formed and distinct from one another; when eaten, you'll feel each tiny egg with your tongue. Pressed caviar, which consists of high-quality eggs too fragile, immature, or bruised to become malossol, has a different texture than fresh—it's chewier. Pressed caviar may consist of a blend of beluga, osetrova, and sevruga; it's been traditionally far less expensive than malossol, but as Caspian caviar becomes increasingly difficult to import, the cost of pressed caviar has risen correspondingly.

Pasteurized caviar consists of whole eggs, not of the highest quality, pasteurized in jars or cans. It keeps longer this way. Because the pasteurization process slightly cooks the caviar, it is chewier than its fresh counterpart.

Serving Caviar. Serve caviar in the same glass container in which it was purchased, placing it in a larger glass bowl filled with ice. This serves two purposes: it keeps the caviar cold, thus retarding spoilage; and it's aesthetic, since the tiny dark pearls of caviar are especially beautiful nestled within the clear shards of ice. Also, use only very small glass, ivory, or wooden spoons and knives; metal implements impart a metallic taste to the eggs.

As far as accompaniments, there are two points of view—ascetic and decadent. Ascetics feel caviar should be accompanied by nothing more than a dry piece of toast made from excellent bread. Decadents offer a variety of accompaniments. Most popular is the duo of chopped cooked egg and finely chopped raw onion placed in individual glass bowls. If you're a decadent, don't feel confined to white bread: fine pumpernickel, black or rye add an interest of their own (do toast them and remove the crusts, however).

. . . and Champagne

True champagne is created from legally specified grapes grown in limited, defined sections of the French province Champagne. It is fermented entirely in its original bottle. Top-quality French labels include Dom Perignon, Bollinger, Tattinger, Heidsieck Monopole, Louis Roederer, Veuve Clicquot, Krug, Perrier Jouet, and Phillipponnat. All other bubbly wines—including the many excellent, first-rate varieties made in the United States—are technically called sparkling wines.

Champagne is at its best when served chilled—but not too chilled. To open without wasting the wine, tilt the bottle at a slight angle and rock the cork slowly back and forth: it will ease out smoothly. Serve in slender flute glasses.

1928

In the United States

Première of George Gershwin's *An American in Paris* . . .
After long and expensive trial in customs court, Brancusi's
Bird in Space is judged a work of art, allowed to enter the
United States duty-free . . . Publication of *The Art of the
Dance* by (the late) Isadora Duncan; *Ryder* by Djuna
Barnes . . .

In Paris

Retired World Heavyweight Champion Gene Tunney
comes to Paris for short visit . . . Zelda Fitzgerald begins
study of ballet . . . Kay Boyle joins Raymond Duncan's
colony dedicated to Greek ideals, vegetarianism, and simplicity . . . Arrivals: American artists Stuart Davis and
Isamu Noguchi, Henry Miller . . . Virgil Thomson composes *Four Saints in Three Acts* based on work by Gertrude
Stein . . . Publication of Djuna Barnes's *Ladies Almanack*
(Contact Editions) . . .

GERALD AND SARA MURPHY:

The Treasure Hunt

*G*erald and Sara Murphy combined in their daily life
the finest traditions of America and France, distill-
ing in the process something rare and special, in-
digenous to neither the old world nor the new.

The Murphys' backgrounds were, though privileged,
conventional enough, and certainly give no clue as to why
or how they ended up setting the quintessential style for
expatriate life in the twenties. Gerald's father founded
Mark Cross, an expensive leather-goods store in New
York; Gerald attended Hotchkiss and graduated from Yale
in 1912,* afterward working for his father.

Sara was born in Cincinnati but spent much of her
childhood in Europe; as a result she spoke fluent French,
German, and Italian. She and her sisters were given an expensive private education, then a presentation at the
Court of St. James. By many accounts they were beautiful,
talented, and the 1914 rage of London.

Married in 1915, the Murphys had the first of three

---

*At Yale Gerald was tapped for Skull and Bones and voted best dressed. One of
his classmates, Cole Porter, remained a close friend for life.

children—a girl, Honoria—two years later; the boys, Patrick and Baoth, quickly followed. In 1917, with the United States in the war, Gerald enlisted and went off to Texas for pilot training. Before he could make it to Europe, the armistice was declared.

Around this time the Murphys grew unhappy with the conservatism they saw slowly creeping across the United States. Like many of their friends, they feared that innovations in art, literature, and music were being stifled in a country that eschewed creative innovation and exalted the commonplace. Passage of the Eighteenth Amendment was the final straw: a nation that could forbid its citizens to take a drink, they thought, was capable of anything. Believing a creative life no longer possible at home, they came in 1921 to Paris.

Soon after their arrival they saw for the first time paintings by Picasso, Braque, and Gris. Gerald was astounded at the combinations of color and form. Deciding on the spot to become a painter, he studied with the Russian artist Natalia Goncharova. Between 1921 and 1929, the year he finished his last canvas, Gerald produced ten paintings. His work—careful, precise renderings of everyday household or mechanical objects—anticipated Pop Art by over forty years.*

Goncharova, a set designer for Diaghilev's ballet, introduced the Murphys to the famed impressario; through

---

*In 1964 the New York Museum of Modern Art held a retrospective of Murphy's work, acquiring one of his canvases for its permanent collection.

him they became friendly with Picasso, Stravinsky, Satie, Cocteau, and others in the modernist scene. Through these contacts Gerald was commissioned to create an "American" ballet, *Within the Quota*, for the Ballet Suédois. Cole Porter wrote the score, which satirized the United States. The set was Gerald's responsiblity, and—with a huge backdrop parodying the front page of a Hearst newspaper—he did a good enough job to win a "*C'est beau, ça*," from Picasso.

Although the Murphys loved Paris and kept an apartment on rue Gît-le-Coeur, they are best known for their life on the Riviera. They first saw the Côte d'Azure when Cole Porter invited them to his rented château in Cap d'Antibes in 1921. In those days the Riviera was deserted in summer; Cap d'Antibes' single hotel closed from June to October for lack of business. So little swimming was done from the beach that it was covered completely by a bed of seaweed four feet thick. The Murphys cleaned away a small corner, large enough to sunbathe; they swam, played on the sand, and met the tiny community's residents. By visit's end they'd found a new home.

Soon they bought a villa high on a hill with a splendid view of Antibes' red tile roofs and the blue Mediterranean. The previous owner had been a French army officer stationed abroad; on trips home he'd brought exotic plants for the garden: date palms, white-leaved Arabian maples, pepper, olive, fig, and lemon trees. There were also flowers—oleander, mimosa, rose, heliotrope, jasmine, camelia, and in the evening there were nightingales. The

The Treasure Hunt

Murphys added a second floor and a sunroof and decorated the villa with wicker furniture, simple area rugs, and plain wooden tables. There were always large vases of flowers from the gardens. They called the place Villa America.

It was here that the Murphys concocted their special blend of two cultures. From the French they took the men's Riviera "uniform" of striped sailor jersey and white duck pants, the rarefied half of the villa's cuisine, the modernist explosion in the arts, wines, and a good many of their friends. From America they took jazz (the drummer in Jimmy Durante's band sent them monthly shipments of the hottest records), modern dance, literature, cocktails, negro spirituals, a simpler cuisine, and the rest of their friends. Over time the "Murphy Blend" was enjoyed by, among others: Dorothy Parker, Robert Benchley, Cole Porter, Rudolph Valentino, Pablo and Olga Picasso, Stravinsky, Alexander Woollcott, Fernand Léger, Ernest and Pauline Hemingway, Erik Satie, Scott and Zelda Fitzgerald, John and Katy Dos Passos, and Archibald and Ada MacLeish.

A typical day started with breakfast on the terrace. Later Gerald painted in his detached studio, the children studied with their tutor, and Sara gardened. Before noon the whole family—and whoever was visiting—headed to the beach. In the evening there were cocktails and dinner. Afterward there might be an American movie projected onto a sheet, or music and dancing, or—best of all, according to those who were there—just conversation.

The Murphys' life centered on family—the children were not only included in everything, but were often the reason for a special excursion. One of the best stories in Honoria Murphy Donnelly's book, *Sara & Gerald*, tells of such an event. One summer day the children found a rusted, very old box in the garden. Inside was a faded map, drawn on parchment, of the French coast: near St. Tropez, a cross had been drawn in what appeared to be blood. Shown the map, Gerald and Sara were every bit as excited as their children. The map was authentic, they said, and the cross surely indicated buried treasure!

For days the children studied the map with mounting exhilaration as Gerald and Sara readied their sloop, *Honoria*, for a treasure sail. Sara prepared food, and Gerald bought two tents so they could camp on the beach at the sign of the cross. Part of the fun was keeping the treasure hunt a secret to outsiders, so when friends asked where they were going, the Murphys—parents and children alike—turned mysterious: "Just for a pleasure cruise."

Finally the day of departure arrived and the family sailed from Villa America, the treasure map under careful guard. At noon they dropped anchor and went swimming. Then, as Honoria later described:

> After we had climbed back on board the *Honoria*, Mother laid out huge beach towels in the cockpit, and we wrapped ourselves in them. She then put a piece by Stravinsky on the crank-up gramophone, and we had a delicious lunch of gnocchi, salad, and

fresh peaches with cream. We went below for naps, as the boat got under way. That night, we put into the port of St. Tropez and tied up at the municipal dock. We took a walk through the town, and when we returned a crowd had gathered. There were friendly cries, "*Ce sont des Américains.*" Americans were still a rarity on the Riviera in 1928.

The next day they arrived at the cove near St. Tropez, and that night camped on the beach and told ghost stories to the accompaniment of spooky music from the crank-up gramophone. Next morning, following an early breakfast, the treasure hunt began. Gerald and the children walked up and down the beach, checking the lay of the land with the map. When Gerald shouted that he'd found the spot, they dug, uncovering an old metal box which looked much too small to contain buried treasure. Inside was another piece of parchment directing them to a spot further down the beach. Here, at long last, the children found the pirate chest. Inside were costume jewels and beads—"rubies," "diamonds," "emeralds"—and old compasses, coins, earrings, and bracelets.

Gerald and Sara had, of course, planned the entire episode, finding parchment paper and an old chest in Paris and buying the treasure at flea markets and junk shops. "It was years later," Honoria wrote in 1982, "that we learned the treasure hunt had been invented. I still wear the 'ruby' necklace."

*

The Found Meal for Gerald and Sara Murphy

GNOCCHI À LA VIRGIL THOMSON
SALADE VERTE
FRESH PEACHES WITH CREAM

Gnocchi à la Virgil Thomson

> Virgil Thomson's personal recipe for gnocchi
> —included in *The Alice B. Toklas Cook Book*—
> inspired the version found here.

Thinly slice ½ pound fontina cheese, place in bowl, and cover with milk. Set aside while preparing gnocchi.

Drop 2 pounds peeled white potatoes into boiling, salted water and cook until tender when pierced with knife, approximately 40 minutes. Drain potatoes and put through a ricer (or mash them). Blend in beaten egg. Continue to mix while adding, bit by bit, ¾ to 1 cup white flour. Mix until dough forms into ball that holds together. Divide dough into pecan-sized pieces, pressing each against tines of fork to give texture. Gnocchi should be olive-shaped, longer than wide.

Drop gnocchi, a few at a time, into pan of boiling, salted water; they will rise to the top when cooked, about 3 to 5 minutes. While they're cooking, remove fontina from milk, placing a layer of fontina and a tablespoon of butter on bottom of serving bowl. Cover cheese with layer of hot, drained gnocchi; cover gnocchi with more cheese and butter; continue layering gnocchi and cheese, ending with a layer of cheese on top. Mix gently. Serve.

Salade Verte

A simple green salad with a tart vinaigrette would go best with the rich and creamy gnocchi. A recipe for green salad is given on page 185.

Fresh Peaches with Cream

Wash peaches well. Peel. Slice even sections into bowl; cover with fresh cream. Serve.

ZELDA FITZGERALD:

Pearl Soup

One day when Zelda Fitzgerald was a little girl she called the fire department, reported a child stuck on a roof, and gave her own address. When she hung up she climbed to the roof, kicked away the ladder, and leaned back to enjoy the ensuing commotion on sleepy, tree-lined Pleasant Avenue in Montgomery, Alabama. Below her gathered screaming fire engines and worried firemen, delighted children, and curious neighbors, wondering just what trouble the judge's daughter had gotten into now.

What else can you expect from a girl named after a wild gypsy queen in a novel? People who knew Zelda as a child said she'd do anything: plunge into the most dangerous waters, climb the highest trees, speak her mind with brutal honesty. In her teens the wildness and daring didn't fade away—they intensified, as did her blonde, hawk-like beauty and cunning wit. This combustible combination of charms proved fatal to young men, for Zelda, though still in high school, was Queen Heartbreaker on the top southern campuses. When war brought an inrush of young officers to Montgomery's Camp Sheridan, her popularity soared. Flyboys performed stunts over her home so often that townspeople complained to the camp's commanding officer. In one summer she collected a cigar box full of soldiers' insignia, the wartime equivalent of a fraternity pin. At country club dances she was mobbed by college boys and second lieutenants, all fighting for a glance, a dance—maybe even a kiss.

It was at such a dance that second lieutenant Scott Fitzgerald rested eyes on eighteen-year-old Zelda Sayre for the first time. Attending a table of superior officers, Fitzgerald's glance fell on a group of young men surrounding a beautiful girl dressed in white, and from the first moment, "I simply had to have her." Oblivious to his duties he walked up to Zelda and introduced himself. That night he wrote in his diary that he had fallen in love.

Zelda felt the same, later writing of a love so intense that her beloved became "distorted in her vision, like pressing her nose upon a mirror and gazing into her own eyes." There was more truth in that than she perhaps realized. Like Zelda, Scott loved to shock others and turn attention to himself. At the start Zelda was the more daring, but soon they became one in a constant search for adventure. They were, Zelda would say, "excitement-eaters."

They married in 1920, shortly after publication of Scott's first novel. *This Side of Paradise,* an overnight bestseller, crystallized the rebelliousness of the postwar generation. Here for the first time were the wild vamps—soon to be called flappers—who did as they pleased while burning candles at both ends. Here were the disillusioned young men home from the war. Here was the new music, the fast talk about art and writing, the feeling of pointlessness for anything but living in the moment. "America was going on the greatest, gaudiest spree in history," Scott wrote. The Jazz Age had begun, and he and Zelda—young, famous, reckless—became its embodiment.

For nearly ten years they played the role of gilded youth. At first their pranks were amusing, almost innocent—diving into the Plaza fountain, riding atop taxicabs. But as the years went by and the drinking increased, their search for pleasure grew destructive and suicidal. There were Zelda's overdoses, Scott's bar-room brawls, week-long binges ended by waking in another city—another country!—wondering how they'd got there.

There was also the matter of work. Constant partying made it difficult and often impossible for Scott to write, but their spendthrift ways made writing imperative. Fitzgerald earned an estimated $100,000 in the four years following publication of his first book—a lot of money in those days; yet they were constantly in debt, always borrowing against future earnings. His second book, *The Beautiful and Damned* (1922) received unfavorable notice and sold below expectations; *The Great Gatsby*, published in 1925, was critically acclaimed but sold poorly. Scott was thus driven to churn out quick and often-mediocre short stories for magazines like *The Saturday Evening Post* or *College Life*.

Zelda, who wanted recognition of her own, began a desperate quest for something to do. In 1928, at the age of

28, she took up ballet with frenzied abandon, neglecting her home, her daughter Scottie, and Scott. Scott was far from an enlightened husband,* as a passage from Zelda's intensely autobiographical novel, *Save Me the Waltz*, indicates. When asked by her husband why she no longer goes carousing with him at night, she replies that doing so keeps her from working the next day; he dismisses her comments as a "female whine."

In 1930 Zelda had a nervous breakdown and entered a sanatorium. When released she turned her back on ballet, taking up painting and writing instead. She had been writing for some time, actually, publishing a few stories now and then in *College Life*—but to sell them she'd had to claim Scott as co-author or let them be published under his name alone. This must have been galling for Zelda as she sought an identity of her own. Canadian writer Morley Callaghan remembered meeting her in the late twenties and hearing her say, repeatedly, "I write prose. It's good prose."

Many blame Zelda for the couple's problems. Scott's biographer Andrew Turnbull viewed her as spoiled, unstable, and incredibly selfish, a life-long drain on his creativity. Ernest Hemingway was convinced that Zelda was the cause of Scott's ruin. He thought Zelda was crazy, and that Scott was blinded by his love of her—and by alcoholism.

But there are many who take Zelda's side. Her biogra-

---

*Fitzgerald was once quoted in a newspaper as saying that "just being in love, really in love—doing it well—is work enough for a woman."

pher, Nancy Milford, saw Zelda as courageous in her passionate pursuit to find work of her own, whereas Scott, Milford felt, was immature and selfish about sharing the limelight. Morrill Cody, who knew both Fitzgeralds in Paris, blamed Scott for Zelda's problems: "she wrote short stories that compared favorably with those of Scott. Her one novel, the largely autobiographical *Save Me the Waltz*, shows that she had a real talent which might have been outstanding if she had been allowed to develop it. Had Scott been more understanding, more intelligent about her, the two would have made a wonderful literary team, in my opinion."

Zelda's greatest literary effort was *Save Me the Waltz*, a novel she wrote while in and out of mental hospitals between 1931 and 1932. Written in a fast-paced, impressionistic style, it's a thinly disguised autobiography about growing up in the south and life in expatriate France. Her heroine is named for her home state, Alabama; Scott—David Knight in the book*—becomes a famous painter. Zelda's intense struggle to become a ballerina is recounted, although her fictional counterpart succeeds.

Without telling Scott, Zelda sent the finished book off to his editor at Scribner's, Maxwell Perkins. Because of the story's autobiographic nature, Perkins felt he couldn't

---

*His original name in the novel was Amory Blaine—the same name as the protagonist of Scott's first novel, *This Side of Paradise*. Under intense pressure from Scott, Zelda changed the name.

Pearl Soup

publish it without letting Scott have a look at it. Scott was devastated by Zelda's portrayal of him and their marriage, considering much of what he read an insult. Perkins agreed, and the two men pressured Zelda to revise the book. She did, making Knight's character so innocuous that he becomes a nonentity. Thus the book becomes all about Alabama's struggle to change from a carefree southern belle into an independent woman. Though Zelda didn't succeed with these goals in her life, the book leaves no doubt how much she wanted to. As such, it's the only self-defense she left behind.

Though it had some good reviews, *Save Me the Waltz* was largely ignored. Scribner's gave it little promotion and in 1932, with the Depression in full swing, most people weren't interested in reading about southern belles and jazz babies. Too, there's an element of the bizarre in the book, an almost surreal undertone that's a bit worrisome (and perhaps a reflection of Zelda's mental instability). The following passage, in which Alabama treats an impoverished ballet-school chum to lunch at the expensive Prunier's, is a good example:

> Secretively Stella extracted whatever it was she dredged from the bottomless soup. She was too engrossed to answer. She was as absorbed as a person searching for a dead body.
>
> "What on earth are you doing, ma chère?" It irritated Alabama that Stella was not more enthusiastic.

She resolved never to take another poor person to a rich man's place; it was a waste of money.

"Sh—sh—sh! Ma chère Alabama, it is pearls I have found—big ones, as many as three! If the waiters know they will claim them for the establishment, so I make a cache in my napkin."

"Really," asked Alabama, "show me!"

"When we are in the street. I assure you it is so. We will grow rich, and you will have a ballet and I will dance in it."

. . . In the pale filtrations of the street they opened the napkin carefully.

. . . Alabama inspected the globular yellow deposits.

"They're only lobster eyes," she pronounced decisively.

Zelda would spend the rest of her life in mental institutions or in her mother's Montgomery home. She painted a great deal, gardened, and occasionally saw Scott. Though they no longer lived together after the early thirties, they remained married and exchanged loving letters until Scott's death from a heart attack at the age of forty-five. Zelda died in a fire at Highland Psychiatric Hospital near Asheville, North Carolina, in 1948.

*

The Found Meal for Zelda Fitzgerald

Bouillabaisse à la Marseillaise

Purists say a true bouillabaisse can only be made in the Marseilles-Toulon region with its large fishing fleets bringing catches of saint-pierre, chapon, rascasse, and girelle into port. The bouillabaisse recipe given here is similar to that of Marseilles, though lacking the fish found only in the Meditererranean. Bouillabaisse needs very little in the way of accompaniment—a crusty baguette and a good bottle of wine will do just fine.

To serve 10 to 12 people, cut 6 to 7 pounds of fish into uniform pieces. Use as wide a selection of flavors and textures as possible, choosing from monkfish, flounder, sole, rock cod, shark, haddock, perch, scrod, snapper, sea bass, whiting, shrimp, and conger eel. Choose also a spiny lobster, cut lengthwise down the middle, or 1 to 2 crabs divided into pieces.

In the bottom of a very large pot, place 1 large minced onion; the chopped white part of 3 leeks; 5 minced garlic cloves; 3 large peeled, seeded, and chopped tomatoes; a small slice of fennel; 1 bay leaf; a 1- to 2-inch piece of dry orange peel; a sprig of thyme; a good pinch of saffron; and, if you like, a dash of Pernod. Salt and pepper to taste. Pour over everything ½ cup high-quality olive oil. Now add fish: first the lobster or crab; then firm-fleshed varieties such as shark and eel (add soft-fleshed fish later). Shake pan vigorously to coat the fish with the oil. Add enough fish stock (see recipe, below) or water to cover vegetables and fish completely. Cover pan and bring to boil; cook briskly 5 to 6 minutes. Add soft-fleshed fish and shrimp and continue boiling another 6 to 8 minutes. Total cooking time should not exceed 15 minutes.

Slice day-old French bread into thick slices, allowing 3 to 4 slices for each diner. Put 1 slice into each diner's soup bowl; put the remainder in a basket on the table. Carefully remove the fish from the pot and arrange it attractively on a platter; place on table. Strain the broth into a deep soup tureen, bring tureen to table and ladle from it a bit of broth over the bread in each soup bowl. Your guests will take it from there.

Fish Stock

Combine in large pot 4 pounds fish heads and bones; include some lobster or crab shells if possible. Cover completely with water. Add 1 bay leaf, 6 sprigs parsley, 1 chopped onion. Salt and pepper to taste. Bring to boil and let simmer, uncovered, 30 minutes. Strain broth through colander lined with cheesecloth. Discard vegetables and fish.

1929

In the United States

Stockmarket crashes October 23; within weeks unemployment rises from half a million to 3.1 million . . . Harry Crosby murders his lover and then commits suicide in New York City . . . *Fifty Million Frenchmen*, with music by Cole Porter, opens on Broadway . . . Elmer Rice wins the Pulitzer Prize for his play *Street Scene* . . . Publication of *A Farewell to Arms* by Ernest Hemingway . . . Founding of New York's Museum of Modern Art . . .

In France

Crash means lack of money for Americans abroad; almost everyone returns home; among those staying on: Gertrude Stein, Sylvia Beach, Natalie Barney, Kay Boyle, Djuna Barnes . . . First issue of Edward Titus's *This Quarter* . . . *The Education of a French Model* by Kiki published in France; Hemingway says publication marks end of the era . . . Hart Crane jailed after argument with Madame Select and attack on arresting policeman . . . Lee Miller, former Vogue model, arrives in Paris in the summer;

eventually apprentices as photographer to Man Ray . . .
Black Sun Press publishes *Short Stories* by Kay Boyle . . .
Death of Sergei Diaghilev (in Venice) . . . Simone de
Beauvoir and Jean Paul Sartre meet at the Sorbonne . . .

KAY BOYLE:

Vegetation

Born in 1903, Kay Boyle was a young whipper-
snapper compared to the rest of her Parisian contemporaries.* In 1914, for instance, when Boyle
was eleven, Djuna Barnes was enjoying a successful journalistic career; John Dos Passos and e. e. cummings were
discovering modernistic writing at Harvard; and Gerald
Murphy was in New York City, graduated from college and
already bored with his work at Mark Cross, Ltd.

And yet, in a way, Boyle had a head start on all these
people. Boyle was born into an affluent midwestern family, and both her mother and grandmother were strong-
minded individualists and early feminists who felt that art
and literature were essential aspects of life. When Boyle
was eleven, her mother read portions of Gertrude Stein's
Tender Buttons to a meeting of doctors; a few years later
she read from *Ulysses* to a Cincinnati labor organization.
Whether the doctors and laborites enjoyed the readings is
beside the point; what matters is that Boyle grew up taking
such writing for granted.

---

*Of the principals in *Found Meals*, only Boyle and Zelda Fitzgerald were born in
this century.

In 1922 Boyle came to France with her new husband, Robert Brault, a French exchange student she'd met in New York while working for the literary magazine *Broom*. They'd planned to visit his parents for the summer before returning to New York, but they stayed on, settling in Brittany. Boyle got to Paris now and then, albeit briefly. On one trip she was so thrilled to meet Robert McAlmon, who symbolized for her all that was best about the Parisian expatriate life she dreamed of having, that she ran away when they were introduced.

Boyle's first five years in France could have filled several novels—and, in fact, did. Her experiences as a young American woman suddenly thrust into a disapproving, bourgeois French family are detailed in *Plagued by the Nightingale*. *Gentlemen, I Address You Privately* captured the daily life of Le Havre and Harfleur. Leaving her husband for a love affair with Ernest Walsh, the tubercular editor of *This Quarter*—as well as Walsh's subsequent death, the later birth of their child, and Boyle's complex, difficult relationship with Walsh's patron and co-editor, Ethel Moorhead—form the basis of *Year Before Last*.

Finally, in 1928, Boyle arrived in Paris where she landed a job ghost-writing the memoirs of a former princess. She met Eugene Jolas, co-editor of *transition*, and through him made friends with the Left Bank literati: James Joyce, Gertrude Stein, Archibald MacLeish, Sylvia Beach. She met McAlmon again, and a sound friendship developed which would last until his death.

Enter Raymond Duncan, brother of Isadora, who

strode about Paris in flowing Greek robes and sandals, a wreath of bay leaves crowning his head. Duncan headed a "colony" outside Paris, an experimental community that supposedly lived by the ideals of ancient Greece. Among other ventures, colonists ran a store selling Greek weavings produced on Duncan's looms.

The idealistic Boyle joined the colony in 1928, inspired by Duncan's vision of communality and his promise of help in her quest to publish finely made books of poetry. Before long she realized that the weavings were actually Greek imports and that the community's real reason for existence was the glorification and profit of Raymond Duncan. When she tried to leave, her infant daughter was held as ransom. Eventually Robert McAlmon cooked up a scheme to kidnap Boyle's daughter from the colony. When this was accomplished, she went into hiding at Harry and Caresse Crosby's country place, Moulin du Soleil. Once her fear of Duncan's retaliation had receded, she moved into Paris.

Boyle wrote an autobiographical short story about this period, *Art Colony*. In it a young woman comes back to her squalid communal living quarters to find herself alone but for a newcomer, an old Russian woman who has come to take shelter. The Russian stares about the cold, dirty rooms and talks of having once seen the sister of Sorrel, the colony's leader:

> "Hell, the sister'd come into the room in Germany when Sorrel had the colony. Set down a bottle of

whiskey and a beefsteak thicker than your arm, and say hell, Sorrel, to hell with your vegetation! Give these poor guys a meal for a change! He'd stand there and cry, her brother, and then she'd start in crying with him and smoothing him down. But she'd have some one cook her the beefsteak just the same. A good thick one," said the Russian woman eagerly, "running with juice and cooked up with French frieds. I knew how she liked them. It was me that made them right for her sometimes. She loved hollandaise sauce like money, and she'd eat it with a spoon. She used to like to start off with artichokes," said the Russian woman, "and them big American olives—"

The young woman fixes a meal for the Russian who, revived, dreams aloud wistfully of better times; both women know the better times will never come. The story is bleak and cold.

Boyle's first book, a collection of short stories, was published in 1929 by the Crosbys' Black Sun Press. In 1930 one of her stories appeared for the first time in *The New Yorker*, commencing an association that would last decades. The list of Boyle's novels and short story collections is endless; she also wrote essays, poetry, and journalism, translated, and taught for many years at San Francisco State University. When Kay Boyle died in late 1992, she was perhaps the last surviving member of the Lost Generation.

*

The Found Meal for Kay Boyle

ARTICHOKE WITH HOLLANDAISE SAUCE
PAN-BROILED STEAK
FRENCH FRIEDS

Whole Boiled Artichoke

Prepare 4 artichokes for boiling by cutting stalk close to choke's rounded bottom, pulling off hard outer leaves, and evenly trimming the rest with scissors. Put base downward in a large pot of boiling salted water. Water should remain at consistent but slow boil throughout cooking. Cook until done, approximately 30 minutes; stem will pierce easily when pressed with a knife. Drain on cloth bottom side up. Serve warm or cold with hollandaise sauce.

Hollandaise Sauce

Divide 1 stick of butter into thirds. In the top of a double boiler set over hot but not boiling water, gently stir together 4 eggs yolks and ⅓ of the butter until butter is melted. Add second ⅓; when melted, add last ⅓ butter, stirring constantly. Remove top of double boiler and beat butter/egg mixture with small wire whisk for 2 or more minutes. Add 1 tablespoon barely warmed lemon juice or white wine vinegar, a little at a time, whisking constantly.

Adjust taste with salt, white pepper and, if desired, a tiny pinch of cayenne. Replace pan over hot water and beat an additional 2 minutes. Serve immediately.

Pan-Broiled Steak

> The steak is based on a 1920s recipe of the famous chef Pampille, whose cookbook, *Les Bons Plats de France*, was popular in France at that time.

For two people, take a 1-pound porterhouse, T-bone, or sirloin steak. Cut off excess fat. Rinse steak in cold water and pat dry with paper towels. In a heavy skillet, place 2 tablespoons butter; place over medium heat until melted and hot (a single drop of water flicked into the pan will sizzle vigorously). Throw in a few thin slices of onion, followed by steak. Sauté steak for 3 to 4 minutes on one side; turn and sauté until steak is done to your taste. When you see a little red juice seeping at the surface, it is rare. Continue cooking longer if you desire your steak medium or well done. When done, add ½ cup beef stock and 1 tablespoon wine vinegar to pan, turn steak once, and place on heated plate. Garnish with onions. Reduce stock in pan to 1 or 2 tablespoons and drizzle onto steak. Salt and pepper to taste.

French Fries

Peel and cut 4 large baking potatoes into long sticks no wider than ½ inch. Place in bowl and cover with cold water for 10 to 15 minutes. Remove and dry by wiping with a towel. Fill deep (4- to 5-quart) pot half full of vegetable oil and heat *very slowly* until a small cube of bread, dropped into the fat, browns in exactly 60 seconds. The oil will be just below smoking point—perfect for frying potatoes. Drop in generous handful of potatoes; oil will bubble, sputter, hiss, and gradually die down. Let potatoes fry about 2 minutes, or until the oil has stopped its lively activity. If using wire basket, lift potatoes out and drain on paper towels; if not, lift out with slotted spoon. Allow oil to regain hot temperature, and throw in another handful of potatoes. Continue cooking this way until all potatoes are drained on paper towels. Allow to cool 5 minutes.

Allow oil to reheat. Fry potatoes by handfuls once more, about 3 minutes this time. When a nice golden brown, remove potatoes and drain on paper towels. Serve immediately.

1930

In the United States

Sinclair Lewis wins Nobel Prize for Literature . . . Publication of *The 42nd Parallel* by John Dos Passos; *The Bridge* by Hart Crane; *New Found Land* by Archibald MacLeish; *My Thirty Years' War* by Margaret Anderson

In Paris

Elmer Rice returns to do research for play, *The Left Bank* . . . Henry Miller returns to Paris

ELMER RICE:

Candide's Garden with Turnips

€ lmer Rice no sooner graduated from New York Law
School and won admittance to the bar than he decided he'd rather be a playwright. A little crazy,
maybe, but it worked: his first play, *On Trial,* was a smash
hit, opening on Broadway to both critical and public acclaim. Only twenty-one, he was that happiest of clichés:
rich and famous overnight. His next play, *The Adding Machine,* was also successful. Following on the heels of these
two brilliant starts, however, came a series of disasters.
Hoping a change of scene would stimulate his creativity,
Rice and his family came to Paris in 1925.

Rice was not the average expatriate writer. For one
thing, he was a financially secure family man. For another,
he'd already tasted success. And for yet another, he didn't
think exile was the answer to the unsatisfying intellectual
climate in America. He certainly didn't consider *himself* in
exile; he was merely traveling, he said, and it was true.
Using Paris as a base, the Rices gradually toured France,
later visiting Switzerland, England, Italy, Germany, and
Austria. When not traveling he worked on a new play, *Life
Is Real.*

In Paris Rice visited the cafés popular with Americans, but not habitually. He formed acquaintances with a few American writers—Dos Passos, cummings, Hemingway, and Sherwood Anderson among them—but for the most part kept his distance. Someone threw a party for Rice and the Montparnasse gang came, but they would come to anything. Samuel Putnam recalled that even though nobody knew who Elmer Rice was, more than a hundred people came to a vodka party in his honor and squeezed into two closet-sized rooms. "I can still see the bewildered look on Mr. Rice's face," Putnam wrote, "as he stood there squeezed against the wall."

After two years Rice returned to New York and, as he'd hoped, the change had been good for him. A play on which he collaborated with Philip Barry, *Cock Robin,* opened on Broadway in 1928; *The Subway* opened in 1929, the same year he won the Pulitzer for *The Street Scene.*

Rice returned to Paris in 1930 to reacquaint himself with the Latin Quarter for a play he was writing, *The Left Bank.* The Quarter had changed completely since his first visit in 1925 at the apex of the expatriate scene. By 1930 the expats had fallen prey to the Crash of 1929; few Americans were left, and those who remained seemed dazed and bitter. *Les années folles* were over.

Rice described *The Left Bank* as "a story about the expatriates, a study in the psychology of escapism and an affirmation of the belief that one can solve one's problems only by facing them." In it he attacks the double standard of sexual mores, the paucity of American culture, and the overwhelming Puritanism controlling society. He calls America "a cultural desert," but continues to insist that one must stay there and fight the battle for change.

His vehicle for all this is an American couple, John and Claire, who have lived for years in a series of cheap Paris hotels. In the play's first act, Claire begins to question the necessity of staying away from her own country; John refuses to return. Other disaffections throughout the play—not the least of which is John's most recent casual affair—help Claire decide in the final act that she must divorce him and return home. She's tired of exile, she says, tired of drifting. She wants to go back to her roots and live among her own people. John argues with her, but she stands firm. Her vision of her future is reminiscent of Candide in his garden:

JOHN: We are living in the most civilized country that there is in the world today—and you call it living in exile!

CLAIRE: Yes, that's just it! We're living in the midst of it, without ever becoming a part of it. We're aliens here and we'll never be anything else. And all the people we know; they're all aliens too—playing around on the outside of something they can never make their own. We're like a lot of hungry little children, pressing our noses against a shop-window and crying for delicacies that we can never touch. I've

Candide's Garden with Turnips

had enough of it. I want to go home and dig for turnips in my own garden.

✶

The Found Meal for Elmer Rice

TRUITE GRENOBLOISE À LA MODERNE
TURNIPS À LA CHAMPENOISE
OMELET AU KIRSCH
WINE

Truite Grenobloise à la Moderne

This recipe was inspired by the culinary reminiscences of A. J. Liebling, the late *New Yorker* journalist who lived in Paris in his (and the century's) mid-twenties. When his wealthy father visited in 1927, Liebling talked him into a dinner at Maillabuau's, one of Paris's best restaurants, where they feasted on, among many other dishes, Truite Grenobloise. In later years, looking back on that year abroad, Liebling said, "if I had compared my life to a cake, the sojourn in Paris would have presented the chocolate filling. The intervening layers were plain sponge."

The court bouillon in which to poach the trout may be prepared a day or two in advance. Combine in a saucepan 1 small minced onion, 1 minced shallot, 1 finely chopped carrot, 1 finely chopped celery stalk, and 3 tablespoons butter. Cook slowly over moderate heat until vegetables have become soft (do not brown!). Add 3 cups dry white wine, 3 cups water, 2 tablespoons lemon juice, a bouquet garni (composed of a few sprigs of thyme and parsley and 1 bay leaf), 1 tablespoon salt, and a dozen whole peppercorns. Bring to a boil and let simmer briskly for 15 to 20 minutes. Pour through a finely meshed sieve. Store in refrigerator until ready for use.

Clean 4 medium-sized trout, leaving heads and tails intact. Place in a pan large enough to hold all 4 fish comfortably, and cover with cooled court bouillon. Bring just to simmer over medium heat (bubbles should not break the surface) and let trout cook until done, approximately 12 minutes or until eyeballs turn white. Drain and arrange on serving platter.

While fish is cooking, heat together in a small pan 2 minced shallots, 1½ cups dry champagne, a pinch of salt, and a scant grind of pepper. Bring to simmer and add 1½ cups cream and 4 tablespoons tomato purée. Cook sauce gently until it thickens, stirring occasionally—it should never boil. When sauce thickens, it is ready: beat in another tablespoon or 2 of champagne, adjusting consistency to taste, and whisk vigorously. Strain through finely meshed sieve, pour over trout, and serve.

Turnips à la Champenoise

Wash, peel, and cube 2 pounds of turnips. Blanch in boiling water for about 5 minutes, remove from water, and drain thoroughly. Add ¼ pound diced bacon into still-boiling water, simmering gently for 4 minutes. Drain bacon and pat dry with kitchen towel. In saucepan with tight-fitting lid, sauté bacon with ½ cup chopped onion in 1½ tablespoons butter until lightly browned. Sprinkle 1 tablespoon flour over mixture, and blend thoroughly. Remove from heat and stir in 1 cup beef broth, a few grinds of fresh pepper, the zest of 1 lemon, and 1 tablespoon fresh basil. Return to heat and bring to simmer. Stir in turnips. Cover and simmer until turnips are tender, about 30 minutes. Remove cover, and simmer until sauce becomes thick. Just before serving sprinkle with chives.

Omelet au Kirsch

Kirsch omelets were also served the night Liebling brought his father to Maillabuau's.

Make each omelet individually. In a small mixing bowl break 2 eggs. Add a tiny pinch of salt, 1½ teaspoons sugar, ½ teaspoon kirsch, and 1½ tablespoons heavy cream; beat rapidly with a fork until blended. In a French omelet pan melt 1 tablespoon unsalted butter over high heat, coating the pan. Add eggs, spreading them over pan to make a uniform coating. Sprinkle a little grated lemon rind over the eggs. Run a fork around the edge of eggs to free omelet;

fold in thirds just as egg stops being runny. Remove omelet to warmed serving platter. Sprinkle with powdered sugar and place under the broiler briefly (this carmelizes the sugar). Garnish with a brandied cherry or two. Warm 2 tablespoons kirsch, pour over the omelet, and set it alight just before serving.

Suggested Wines

Liebling mentions that a Montrachet was served with the fish. Montrachet is a white burgundy considered by many to be the greatest of all the world's dry white wines; consequently, it's extremely expensive.* You might try, instead—since this meal is meant to celebrate the symbolic return of exiles to America and the tilling of home soil—a fine California chardonnay.

---

*In the first volume of his memoirs, *20th Century Journey: The Start*, the journalist William Shirer fondly recalled perusing the wine list at a place called Rouzier's Rotisserie Périgourdine. Among its bargains: a number of Montrachets priced from two to three dollars.

Candide's Garden with Turnips

AFTERWORD

A nd so it ended.

Common lore blames the finish of the ex-patriate years on the stock market crash, but in truth the Paris scene had been dying for years. By 1925 Americans—lured by cheap ship travel, a lopsided rate of exchange, and stories about the loose bohemian life—had taken over the Left Bank. Those who had arrived in the decade's early years watched with dismay as Paris filled up with tourists, as once-intimate cafés and hangouts grew crowded with strangers hoping to catch a glimpse of Hemingway or Joyce or Stein. The old hands hated the change, complaining bitterly to one another. "Montpar-nasse has ceased to exist," Djuna Barnes mourned to the journalist Wambly Bald. "There is nothing left but a big crowd."

The old gang moved on. Hemingway, disgusted by sycophants and drunks, left for Havana in 1928; though he would visit Paris many times throughout his life, he never lived there again. Isadora Duncan died, Harry Crosby and Hart Crane committed suicide, George An-theil went home and dropped out of sight, Nina Hamnett returned to London. Little by little the golden years lost their glitter.

Then came the Crash, and suddenly the Americans no longer owned Paris. Some stayed. Bob McAlmon remained well into the thirties; Djuna Barnes until the war came along; Natalie Barney and Gertrude Stein until they died. Sylvia Beach, too, stayed on, continuing to run her bookstore until the Germans invaded Paris.

Time passed, and the golden years receded into memory. The expats were scattered now, grown older. A surprising number of the old gang wrote memoirs, wanting to keep the memory of that time alive so that others could know and understand—perhaps be inspired. "We were not so different from those who had preceded us," wrote Harold Loeb, the real-life model for Robert Cohn in *The Sun Also Rises*. "Perhaps our hopes were a little higher, our disappointments deeper: but at least ours was a generation that had set out to discover, a generation that had chosen to dare."

In the end, though, perhaps the Lost Generation wasn't as daring as all that. Perhaps it was only that they'd survived a war and found themselves still alive and young, with no cares or responsibilities in an economy promising to skyrocket forever. Why *not* live in Paris, write poetry, paint pictures, fall in love, shoot for the Great American Novel? Why not live fully and aim for an impossible goal? And if the goal wasn't achieved, well, perhaps it had been enough merely to be there, freely spending youth and stockpiling memories.

Harold Stearns, who wasted his youth in Paris as scandalously as anyone, summed it up best: "It was a useless, silly life," he wrote many years later, "and I have missed it every day since."

BIBLIOGRAPHY

Acosta, Mercedes
    Here Lies the Heart. Reynal & Company: New York, 1960.
Allan, Tony
    Americans in Paris. Chicago: Contemporary Books, 1977.
Allhusen, Dorothy
    A Medley of Recipes. London: Chapman and Hall, 1936.
Anderson, Margaret
    My Thirty Years' War. New York: Covici, Friede, 1930.
Antheil, Georges
    Bad Boy of Music. Garden City, N.Y.: Doubleday, Doran, 1945.
Baker, Carlos
    Ernest Hemingway: A Life Story. New York: Scribner's, 1969.
Baker, Josephine and Bouillon, Jo
    Josephine. New York: Harper & Row, 1977.
Bald, Wambly
    On the Left Bank, 1929–1933; edited by Benjamin Franklin. Athens: Ohio
        University Press, 1987.
Barnes, Djuna
    Ladies Almanack (privately printed in Paris, 1928). Reprinted New York:
        Harper & Row, 1972.
    Nightwood. New York: Harcourt, Brace, 1937.
    Ryder. New York: Liveright, 1928.
Beach, Sylvia
    Shakespeare and Company. New York: Harcourt, Brace, 1959.
Biddle, George
    An American Artist's Story. Boston: Little, Brown, 1939.

Boardman, Bess (ed.)
>   *Sincerely Yours: A Collection of Favorite Recipes of Well-Known Persons.*
>   San Francisco: Grabhorn Press, 1942.

Boylan, James
>   *The World and the 20's.* New York: The Dial Press, 1973.

Boyle, Kay and McAlmon, Robert
>   *Being Geniuses Together.* London: Secker & Warburg, 1938; New York:
>   Doubleday, 1968.

Bricktop, with James Haskins
>   *Bricktop.* New York: Atheneum, 1983.

Brown, Milton W.
>   *The Story of the Armory Show.* Washington, D.C.: The Joseph H. Hirsh-
>   horn Foundation, 1963.

Bryher
>   *The Heart to Artemis: A Writer's Memoir.* New York: Harcourt, Brace,
>   1962.

Callaghan, Morley
>   *That Summer in Paris.* New York: Coward-McCann, 1963.

Carpenter, Humphrey
>   *Geniuses Together.* London: Unwin Hyman, 1987.

Chalon, Jean
>   *Portrait of a Seductress: The World of Natalie Barney.* New York: Crown
>   Publishers, 1979.

Charters, James
>   *This Must Be the Place: Memoirs of Montparnasse.* Edited by Morrill
>   Cody with an Introduction by Ernest Hemingway. London: Herbert
>   Joseph, 1934. New York: MacMillan, 1989.

Cody, Morrill
>   *The Women of Montparnasse* (with Hugh Ford). New York: Cornwall
>   Books, 1984.

Cowley, Malcolm
>   *Fitzgerald and the Jazz Age.* New York: Scribner's, 1966.
>   *Exile's Return.* New York: Viking, 1951.
>   *A Second Flowering.* New York: Viking, 1973.

Crane, Hart
>   *The Letters of Hart Crane.* Berkeley and Los Angeles: University of Cali-
>   fornia Press, 1965.

Crosby, Caresse

> *The Passionate Years.* Carbondale: Southern Illinois University Press, 1968.

Crosby, Harry

> *Shadows of the Sun: The Diaries of Harry Crosby.* Santa Barbara: Black Sparrow Press, 1977.

Curnonsky and Rouff, Marcel

> *The Yellow Guides for Epicures: Paris.* New York, Harper & Brothers, 1926.

Donnelly, Honoria Murphy with Billings, Richard N.

> *Sara & Gerald.* New York: Times Books, 1982.

Dos Passos, John

> *The Best Times: An Informal Memoir.* New York: New American Library, 1966.

> *The Fourteenth Chronicle: Letters and Diaries of John Dos Passos.* Boston: Gambit, 1973.

Duncan, Isadora

> *My Life.* New York: Boni & Liveright, 1927.

Field, Andrew

> *Djuna: The Life and Times of Djuna Barnes.* New York: Putnam's, 1983.

Fitch, Noel Riley

> *Sylvia Beach and the Lost Generation.* New York: W. W. Norton, 1983.

Fitzgerald, F. Scott

> *Tender Is the Night.* New York: Scribner's, 1933.

> *The Letters of F. Scott Fitzgerald,* ed. Andrew Turnbull. New York: Scribner's, 1963.

Fitzgerald, Zelda

> *Save Me the Waltz.* New York: Scribner's, 1932.

Flanner, Janet

> *Paris Was Yesterday.* New York: The Viking Press, 1972.

Ford, Ford Madox

> *It Was the Nightingale.* Philadelphia: Lippincott, 1933.

Ford, Hugh

> *Four Lives in Paris.* San Francisco: North Point Press, 1987.

> *The Left Bank Revisited: Selections from the Paris Tribune, 1917–1934.*

> *Published in Paris.* New York: MacMillan, 1975.

Glassco, John

> *Memoirs of Montparnasse.* New York: Viking Press, 1970.

Hamnett, Nina

    Laughing Torso. New York: Ray Long and Richard R. Smith, 1932

Handbook for Paris and Environs. London: Ward, Lock, 1926.

Hemingway, Ernest

    The Sun Also Rises. New York: Scribner's, 1926.

    A Moveable Feast. New York: Scribner's, 1964.

Hotchner, A. E.

    Papa Hemingway. New York: Random House, 1966.

Huddleston, Sisley

    Back to Montparnasse: Glimpses of Broadway in Bohemia. Philadelphia: J.
        B. Lippincott, 1931.

    Paris Salons, Cafés, Studios: Being Social, Artistic and Literary Memories.
        Philadelphia: J. B. Lippincott, 1928.

Hughes, Langston

    The Big Sea: An Autobiography. New York: Hill and Wang, 1963.

Imbs, Bravig

    Confessions of Another Young Man. New York: Henkle-Yewdale, 1936.

Josephson, Matthew

    Life Among the Surrealists. New York: Holt, 1962.

Klüver, Billy and Martin, Julie

    Kiki's Paris: Artists and Lovers 1900–1930. New York: Harry N. Abrams,
        1989.

Kohner, Frederick

    Kiki of Montparnasse. New York: Stein and Day, 1967.

Liebling, A. J.

    Between Meals: An Appetite for Paris. San Francisco: North Point Press,
        1986.

Loeb, Harold

    The Way It Was. New York: Criterion Books, 1959.

Longstreet, Stephen

    We All Went to Paris: Americans in the City of Light, 1776–1971. New
        York: Macmillan, 1972.

MacLeish, Archibald

    New & Collected Poems, 1917–1976. Boston: Houghton Mifflin, 1976.

Mellow, James R.

    Charmed Circle: Gertrude Stein & Company. New York: Avon Books,
        1974.

Milford, Nancy

    Zelda: A Biography. New York: Harper & Row, 1970.

Mizener, Arthur

    The Far Side of Paradise: A Biography of F. Scott Fitzgerald. Boston: Houghton Mifflin, 1965.

Monnier, Adrienne

    The Very Rich Hours of Adrienne Monnier: An Intimate Portrait of the Literary and Artistic Life in Paris Between the Wars. Translated by Richard McDougall. London: Millington, 1986.

Museum of Modern Art

    Four Americans in Paris: The Collections of Gertrude Stein and Her Family. New York: Museum of Modern Art, 1970.

Newman, E. M.

    Seeing Paris. New York: Funk & Wagnalls, 1931.

Olivier, Fernande

    Picasso et Ses Amis. Paris: Stock, 1933. Translated by Jane Miller under the title Picasso and His Friends. New York: Appleton-Century, 1965.

Porter, Cole

    The Complete Lyrics of Cole Porter, edited by Robert Kimball. New York: Knopf, 1983.

Potts, Willard

    Portraits of the Artist in Exile. Seattle: University of Washington, 1979.

Prin, Alice (Kiki)

    The Education of a French Model. New York: Boar's Head Books, 1950.

Putnam, Samuel

    Paris Was Our Mistress: Memoirs of a Lost and Found Generation. New York: Viking, 1947.

Ray, Man

    Self Portrait. New York: McGraw Hill, 1963.

Reboul, J. B.

    La Cuisinière Provençale. Marseille: Éditions Tacussel, 1887.

Rice, Elmer

    The Left Bank. New York: Samuel French, 1931.

Rogers, W. G.

    When This You See Remember Me: Gertrude Stein in Person. New York: Avon Books, 1973.

Rood, Karen L. (ed.)

    American Writers in Paris, 1920–1939. Detroit: Bruccoli Clark, 1980.

Rubin, William

    The Paintings of Gerald Murphy (catalog for an exhibition). New York: The Museum of Modern Art, 1964.

Scudder, Janet
    Modeling My Life. New York: Harcourt Brace, 1925.
Seldes, George
    Witness to a Century. New York: Ballantine, 1987.
Shirer, William
    20th Century Journey: The Start, 1904–1930. New York: Simon and Schuster, 1976.
Slocombe, George
    Paris in Profile. Boston: Houghton Mifflin, 1929.
Stearns, Harold
    The Confessions of a Harvard Man. New York: Furman, 1935.
    Civilization in the United States. New York: Harcourt, Brace, 1922.
Stein, Gertrude
    The Autobiography of Alice B. Toklas. New York: Harcourt, Brace, 1933.
    Paris France. New York: Scribner's, 1940.
    Picasso. New York: Scribner's 1939.
    The Making of Americans. New York: Something Else Press, 1966.
Street, Julian
    Where Paris Dines. Garden City, N.Y.: Doubleday, Doran, 1929.
Thomson, Virgil
    Virgil Thomson. New York: Knopf, 1966.
Toklas, Alice B.
    The Alice B. Toklas Cook Book. New York: Harper, 1954.
    What Is Remembered. New York: Holt, Rinehart and Winston, 1963.
Tomkins, Calvin
    Living Well Is the Best Revenge. New York: Viking Press, 1971.
Toulouse-Lautrec, Henri and Joyant, Maurice
    The Art of Cuisine. New York: Holt, Rinehart and Winston, 1966.
Turnbull, Andrew
    Scott Fitzgerald. New York: Scribner's, 1962.
    Washboat Days. New York: Orion Press, 1972.
Wickes, George
    The Amazon of Letters: The Life and Loves of Natalie Barney. New York: Putnam's, 1976.
    Americans in Paris, 1903–1939. New York: Doubleday, 1969.
Williams, William Carlos
    The Autobiography of William Carlos Williams. New York: Random House, 1951.

Wilson, Robert
  Paris on Parade. New York: Bobbs-Merrill, 1925.
Wiser, William
  The Crazy Years: Paris in the Twenties. New York: Atheneum, 1983.
Wolff, Geoffrey
  Black Sun: The Brief Transit and Violent Eclipse of Harry Crosby. New
   York: Random House, 1976.
Woon, Basil
  The Paris That's Not in the Guide Books. New York: Brentano's, 1926.

INDEX OF NAMES AND WORKS

INDEX TO RECIPES

Index